Picturing the Past

FINLANDIA UNIVERSITY: 1896 to the Present

Karen S. Johnson
Deborah K. Frontiera
Published by Finlandia University, Hancock, Michigan

Copyright ©2013
by Finlandia University, Hancock, Michigan

All rights reserved. No part of this book may be reproduced or transmitted in any form or by any means, electronic or mechanical, including photocopying or recording by any information storage or retrieval system, without written permission from the publisher.

Finlandia University
Office of Communications
601 Quincy Street
Hancock, Michigan 49930
906-482-5300

Printed in the U.S.A.
ISBN: 978-0-9893484-1-6

Dedication
To all Suomi College and Finlandia University alumni--past, present, and future.

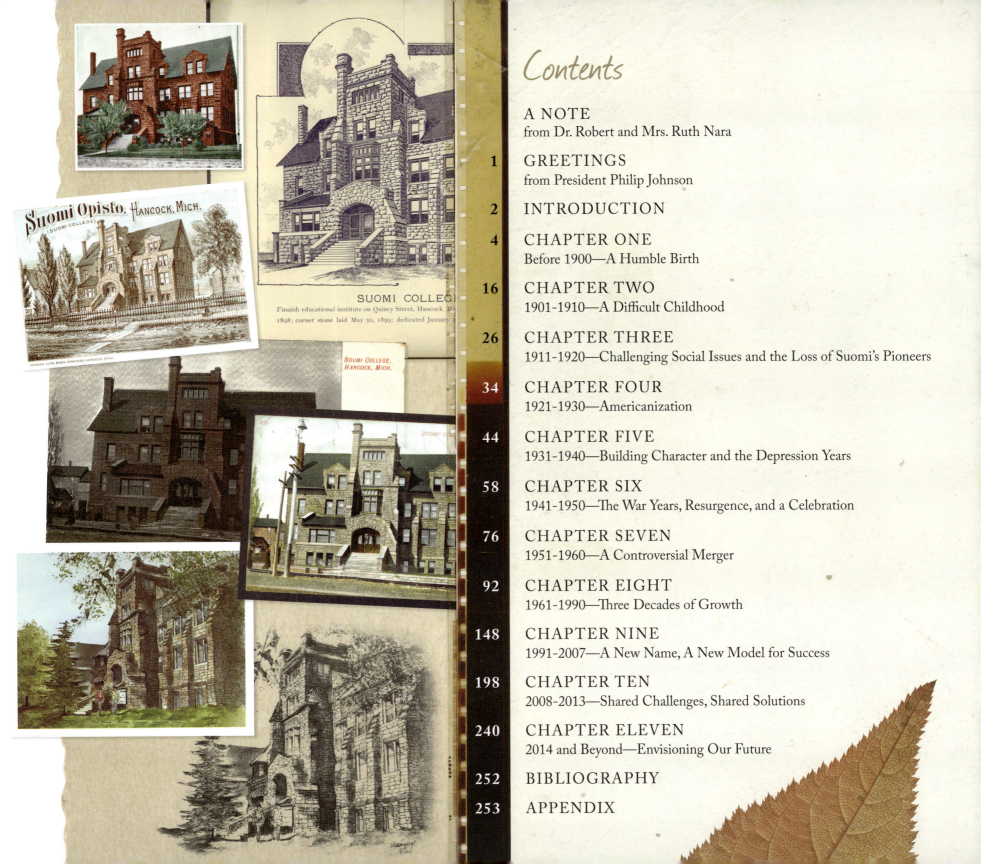

Contents

- **A NOTE** from Dr. Robert and Mrs. Ruth Nara
- **1** — GREETINGS from President Philip Johnson
- **2** — INTRODUCTION
- **4** — CHAPTER ONE: Before 1900—A Humble Birth
- **16** — CHAPTER TWO: 1901-1910—A Difficult Childhood
- **26** — CHAPTER THREE: 1911-1920—Challenging Social Issues and the Loss of Suomi's Pioneers
- **34** — CHAPTER FOUR: 1921-1930—Americanization
- **44** — CHAPTER FIVE: 1931-1940—Building Character and the Depression Years
- **58** — CHAPTER SIX: 1941-1950—The War Years, Resurgence, and a Celebration
- **76** — CHAPTER SEVEN: 1951-1960—A Controversial Merger
- **92** — CHAPTER EIGHT: 1961-1990—Three Decades of Growth
- **148** — CHAPTER NINE: 1991-2007—A New Name, A New Model for Success
- **198** — CHAPTER TEN: 2008-2013—Shared Challenges, Shared Solutions
- **240** — CHAPTER ELEVEN: 2014 and Beyond—Envisioning Our Future
- **252** — BIBLIOGRAPHY
- **253** — APPENDIX

A note from the Näräs

Because this is a history book, we chose a historical photo to include on this page. The photo was taken for the program of the June 1972 Alaska Dental Society meeting, at which Dr. Närä delivered the keynote address, presenting our methods to cure cavities and eliminate gum disease with simple self-help, home-care methods.

The story of Suomi College/Finlandia University is full of people doing what others said could not be done. For that reason, the Närä Foundation chose to support the production of this book.

Dr. Robert and Mrs. Ruth Närä

Närä Foundation — *generosity, common sense and always do the right thing*

Established in 1892 • www.robertnara.com

> "I was a logger and a farmer first. Then a naval officer and a dentist and then I retired and became a logger and a farmer."
> (Bob Närä)

> "The person who says it cannot be done should not interrupt the person doing it."
> (quoted from *The Story of Us* by Bob and Ruth Närä, pg. 87)

> "I recognized years ago that I was the happiest when I was being productive."
> (Ruth Närä)

Greetings from President Philip Johnson

This book tells Finlandia University's story. It belongs among other similar works. The intent here is not to improve or replace. Rather, our hope is that it would meaningfully accompany and, perhaps, enrich Finlandia's memory traditions. It joins a chorus of collections written over the decades. It wishes to sing in harmony, not in unison. Listen for its distinct voice.

Finlandia's story is, of course, a story about people, impassioned people. The following arrangement of texts and photos deepens our appreciation for those who, for 117 years, have been grasped by a vision for education rooted in and sustained by ethnic and spiritual identities, ideas, and commitments.

Generosity has made this book possible. Finlandia University is deeply grateful to Bob and Ruth Nara and the Nara Foundation for their extraordinary financial support and enthusiastic engagement throughout this endeavor. This project would not have happened without them.

Dedicated work by many people has also made this book possible. Very special thanks go to Karen Johnson and Deborah Frontiera. Their ability to blend historical particularity with human peculiarity leaves the reader well informed and also a bit entertained.

The photos evoke. The narratives inform. Enjoy!

Finlandia University president Philip R. Johnson.

Introduction

On behalf of the Finlandia University learning community, thank you for your interest in the history of our school. It is our hope that as you are reading this book and gazing upon the faces and images within, you will sense the enduring spirit of all those who have, for more than a century, nurtured and sustained Suomi College and Finlandia University.

United States immigrant history is rich with courage, purpose, ingenuity, and toil. Suomi College, like many ethnicity-founded institutions of higher learning in North America, was at its core an undertaking meant to preserve and further the faith and culture of its homeland, and to prepare its people for meaningful lives in their new land.

Today, our history and heritage anchor and enrich the Finlandia learning community, even as we respond to and plan for the present and future realities of the 21st century and the needs, expectations, and aspirations of today's students.

The compilation of this book was a considerable task. The result is a "sampler" of sorts, a representative collection of images, quotes, memories, interesting bits of information, and facts. The publication is intended to chronicle the milestone events in the institution's history, convey a sense of the heart and soul of Suomi and Finlandia—and perhaps evoke your own memories.

The foundation on which this book rests comprises terms of presidents, student life and academic programs, new buildings and renovations, and special and recurring events. It is organized by decade, by year, and by presidential terms of office.

The photographs and images within were digitally reproduced from a number of university resources, including the collections of the Finnish American Historical Archive, Suomi College yearbooks, and other Suomi and Finlandia student and institutional publications and records. To convey authenticity and lend visual interest to the book, electronic enhancement of the photographs is minimal.

In the writing of this history, every reasonable attempt has been made to accurately relate key events and essential details. We offer our advance apology for any errors or omissions.

Finlandia University is pleased to acknowledge the generosity of Dr. Robert (Bob) and Mrs. Ruth Nara and the Nara Foundation, the catalysts that sparked this publication.

It also couldn't have been accomplished without the individuals and organizations invested in and passionate about preserving and sharing the Finnish-American immigrant story—past and present—especially James Kurtti, director of the Finlandia University Finnish American Heritage Center and Historical Archive, and archivist Joanna Chopp.

Deborah Frontiera was an enthusiastic champion in the making of this book and her early draft added substantial momentum to the project.

Monte Consulting of Houghton, Michigan, bravely took on the management and graphic design of this book, perhaps not anticipating that it would become a 12-month project. Owner Matt Monte and project manager Ashley Curtis were able, patient, behind-the-scenes stewards of the lengthy publication process.

Graphic artist Lauren (Roell) Schwartz of Monte Consulting, a Class of 2007 alumna of the Finlandia University International School of Art & Design, designed and produced the book's visual layout. Her skill, creativity, and thoughtfulness fill these pages with color and life.

The support and patience of Duane Aho, Finlandia's EVP for external relations, was essential in the completion of this book. President Johnson's confidence in the project was also meaningful.

Our university is small, but along with the Suomi Synod (which founded Suomi College), its spiritual, intellectual, and vocational imprint remains within generations of knowledge-seekers.

Warm regards and happy reading!

Karen S. Johnson
Executive Director of Communications and Marketing
Finlandia University
May 2013

Karen S. Johnson, Editor and Lead Author.

Deborah Frontiera in the Finnish American Historical Archive Reading Room.

A note from Deborah Frontiera

I've been asked many times if I have Finnish ancestors, and I must admit that I do not. I sometimes feel, though, that after writing *Living on Sisu: The 1913 Union Copper Strike Tragedy*, then *Copper Country Chronicler: The Best of J. W. Nara*, and now contributing to this work, that I could be considered an "honorary Finn." I have deep roots in Lake Linden, Michigan, even though I am currently a "seasonal resident." My writing experience spans fiction and non-fiction, adult and children's works, and poetry. Those interested can visit my website at www.authorsden.com/deborahkfrontiera.

There have been many attempts to define the Finnish quality of sisu over the years. One good friend says that when a person runs out of determination and fortitude, sisu is what takes over to get someone through a tough situation (that is, IF that person has sisu). After reading the sources listed in this work's bibliography, and many other documents in the last several years, I have come to define sisu as "true grit with Grace."

Perhaps Suomi College/Finlandia University should have been called the University of Sisu, because through all its ups and downs, periods of brilliant leadership and times of controversy, trial, and change, it has endured!

Deborah K. Frontiera

CHAPTER ONE

Before 1900–A Humble Birth

A copper boom in the mid- to late-1800s and the early 1900s brought tens of thousands of immigrants to the Upper Peninsula of Michigan. Between 1890 and 1910, the area saw a particularly large influx of Finns, most notably from northern Finland, Sweden, and Norway. Faced with inescapable poverty and unemployment, thousands of Finnish men chose to leave their homeland to seek work and better lives in America, bringing with them their families, their faith, and their culture. They worked in the mines and lumber camps, farmed, started businesses of many kinds, and served the spiritual and social needs of their communities.

1876

A. E. Backman.

Rev. A. E. Backman arrived in Hancock, Michigan, to serve as the region's first Church of Finland pastor. Backman's congregation was not, however, the Copper Country's first church to serve Finnish immigrants. In 1867 Swedish, Norwegian, and Finnish immigrants had founded the Scandinavian Evangelical Lutheran Church in Quincy, just north of Hancock. Later, as the Finnish immigrant population increased, the Finns founded their own church in 1873. Nor was Backman's congregation the first exclusively Finnish-speaking church, as followers of the Laestadian movement (also known as Apostolic Lutherans) established a Copper Country congregation in 1873.

Backman found a divided community of Finnish Lutherans: some Laestadian, some loyal to the Church of Finland. He worked with both groups, attempting to reconcile sometimes bitter differences, but "the severity of the climate in the Copper Country and the constant barrage of harassment took its toll on his health" and compelled him to return to Finland.

1885

In January Rev. Juho Kustaa Nikander arrived in Hancock from Finland to serve congregations in Hancock and nearby Calumet and Allouez. Nikander took up the work started by Backman, who returned to Finland in 1883 due to ill health. Rev. J. J. Hoikka, trained at Augustana College and Seminary (Rock Island, Illinois), traveled from Astoria, Oregon, to serve as co-pastor with Nikander.

J. K. Nikander.

In The Story of the Suomi Synod, Jacob W. Heikkinen writes that Nikander was "a 'team person,' a true catalyst, a servant-pastor, an authentic 'foreign missionary' among his kinsmen in the New World." (73)

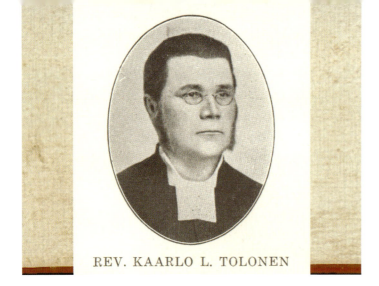

REV. KAARLO L. TOLONEN

Raymond Wargelin writes in Faith of the Finns that "Tolonen was a man of strength and determination, able to mediate difficult situations with great patience and understanding. Without him, Nikander and Hoikka would have been incapable of the achievements of those early days." (333)

1888-1889

In 1888 Rev. K. L. Tolonen, a former missionary to Africa, arrived in Michigan to serve Finnish Lutheran congregations in and around Ishpeming. In 1889, Rev. J. W. Eloheimo traveled from Astoria, Oregon, to serve a pastorate in Calumet. The four Church of Finland pastors now serving the Upper Peninsula met regularly for fellowship and discussion, and in November 1889, with several others, they began plans for the Finnish Evangelical Lutheran Church of America, or Suomi Synod. In December 1889 they adopted a constitution and filed articles of incorporation.

J. J. Hoikka (left), K. L. Tolonen (seated), and J. K. Nikander.

1890-1896

On March 25, 16 people represented nine congregations at the first meeting of the Suomi Synod, in Ishpeming, Michigan. Nikander was elected synod president. Fearing that many immigrant Finns were in danger of becoming "lost to the church" because there were too few pastors to serve them, the new synod's constitution included a provision to found an *opisto*—an institution of learning—to train new pastors. A college committee immediately began drafting preliminary plans and investigating locations. Douglas J. Ollila, Jr., writes in *Faith of the Finns* that "no other effort of the Synod commanded as much attention and interest as Suomi College, and its success in training pastors and laymen assured success of the church itself." (169)

The mission of the opisto, stated in the synod constitution, was "to cultivate a true Christian spirit in its students and to direct them into following Christian principles in their daily living; to give sound training in religion, and in general cultural subjects; to prepare young men for the preaching office by giving instruction and guidance in the arts and knowledge necessary for the calling; to give necessary instruction to those planning on entering the teaching profession; and, insofar as practicable, to prepare its students for other callings." (*Golden Jubilee* 14)

The Suomi Synod and its proposed opisto faced both active and passive opposition. Differences in religious outlook, opposition to an educated ministry, and a mistrust of "Old World" church hierarchy were among the objections. Others didn't see a need to preserve Finnish language and culture in their new land, or didn't believe the Finns could build a school to compare with American schools.

Perhaps most frustrating to college founders was indifference. Arnold Stadius writes in *Finns in North America* that "those concerned with the school's welfare lamented above all the shortsightedness of the Finnish immigrants. A large number were seemingly not interested in the fate of the Finnish college." (101)

Funding the college was a challenge from the beginning, and Nikander and others traveled widely, spreading the word about the college and soliciting donations.

The college competed for students (and donors) with Valparaiso (Illinois) College, Ferris Institute in Big Rapids, Michigan, and other Midwest schools that served immigrants and students of limited means. As well, there were Finnish schools in Calumet (Kansakoulu) and Minneapolis (Kansanopisto), and a number of Finnish correspondence courses.

Determination of the school's location also presented challenges and delayed its opening. Minneapolis and St. Paul, Minnesota; West Superior, Wisconsin; and Marquette, Michigan, were among the communities that expressed interest.

SUPERIORIIN AIJOTTU OPISTO.

An 1894 concept drawing of a proposed Suomi College building in Superior, Wisconsin. A generous verbal commitment of $10,000 to begin building the school did not materialize.

In 1895, at a Suomi Synod convention in Ironwood, Michigan, the school was formally named "Suomi College and Theological Seminary." Finally, at the 1896 synod convention in Calumet, the decision was made to open Suomi College in rented quarters in the Hancock area, home to the largest Finnish population in the Copper Country and fast becoming headquarters of the Suomi Synod.

Nikander was the first Suomi College president and, often, its sole full-time teacher. There is evidence that he took on with some reluctance the additional roles of president and instructor, in addition to his pastoral and synod duties. But Nikander's calling was strong and he answered it energetically and wholeheartedly. He "was in close contact with every student and impressed his personality and his thinking upon them all." (*Finns in North America* 97)

The Finnish Evangelical Lutheran Church (below), built in 1889, still stands on Reservation Street in downtown Hancock. It served congregations until 1966. Left: a glimpse of the interior around 1900.

September 8, 1896

Does not wisdom cry out, And understanding lift up her voice? She takes her stand on the top of the high hill, Beside the way, where the paths meet. (Proverbs 8:1–2)

Suomi College and Theological Seminary was formally dedicated at a worship service at the Finnish Evangelical Lutheran Church in Hancock. Nikander's sermon drew on a reading from Proverbs 8. His concluding remarks looked to the future: "Our college, once it has gotten started and expanded its influence will be a mother that will give birth to smaller schools ... Our more mature students will give inspiring talks in their home communities, and they will conduct summer schools; thus it will be a blessing to our immigrants in many areas." (*Finns in Michigan* 395)

Suomi College students, faculty, and staff gather outside the rented building in West Hancock in which the college began. Later, the building was converted to a public sauna, prompting a tale that Suomi College, like an old-country Finn, was born in a sauna. (Finns in Michigan 395) The building no longer stands.

Eleven students registered for the inaugural term. Following the Christmas holiday, in January 1897, 22 were enrolled; 17 completed the second term. The young men and women ranged in age from their early teens to their late twenties.

Adapted from curricula of the Finnish lyceum and Augustana College, Suomi's original course of study was seven years, followed by a two-year theological course. Years three through six, later to comprise the Academy, were the equivalent of high school grades nine through twelve.

To progress to the next grade level, successful completion of a final spring examination was required. In 1903, the Preparatory Department was formed to serve young children and those requiring basic English and/or Finnish instruction.

Course subjects included religion, Finnish, English, arithmetic, geography, American history, general science, penmanship, drawing, bookkeeping, music, and physical education. Most classes were conducted in the Finnish language, and the majority of the teachers had been educated in Finland.

1897

Enrollment rose to 37, with thirteen second-year students. The faculty was increased to four—two full- and two part-time teachers. Strict order prevailed for the resident students: "up at 5:40 AM, wash face and comb hair before all meals; study, eat, scrub floors; evening prayer service at 9; all in bed at 10 PM." (*Finns in Michigan* 396) Several students who resisted this routine left the school, but enrollment growth continued. The school was quickly outgrowing its rented quarters.

Until December 1899 the college was housed in a rented building on Quincy Street in west Hancock. Classes were held on the first floor. Resident students occupied the second floor, along with the president, and business manager and dean J. H. Jasberg. Tuition was $10 for the winter term, $15 for the spring term. Room and board was $2.00 per week. The 1897 financial report, after one year of operation, showed receipts of $3,312.46 and expenditures of $2,477.31. (*Golden Jubilee* 13) Parents of Suomi College students often paid for their children's tuition with sacks of potatoes or firewood.

1899

On May 30 as many as 2,000 people from Finnish communities in Marquette, the Copper Country, and elsewhere traveled to Hancock for the laying of the cornerstone for the first Suomi College building. The event was described as a "great festival" and railroads offered special trains and reduced fares for the occasion.

The new building and campus occupied three 50-foot lots, each 175 feet deep, on the east side of Quincy Street close to the center of Hancock.

As president of the Suomi Synod, Tolonen presided, saying "I lay this cornerstone for the Suomi College and Theological Seminary building which is to be an institution of higher education for Finnish-American youth in the spirit of Evangelical Lutheranism. No other foundation can be laid than that which has already been laid, which is Jesus Christ." (*Finns in Michigan* 397)

The City of Hancock was represented that day by its mayor, Major A. J. Scott, a distinguished Civil War veteran (and apparently a man with a sense of humor). In his remarks, he said, "As Finns began to migrate to America we thought that they were uneducated and wild like the uncivilized Hottentots of Africa... But here they are founding a college for the education of their youth as well as ours.... Let Marquette have its prison, and Newberry its insane asylum. We have Suomi College." (*Faith of the Finns* 345)

Left: Opisto students in 1897–98.

The date of the groundbreaking for construction of what is now Old Main is uncertain.

Surely, the men who constructed the first Suomi College building, along with the residents of Hancock, took great pride in the impressive sandstone structure, which was completed in just eight months.

The May 30, 1899, laying of the cornerstone for the college's first building was a "great festival." An officially marked cornerstone cannot be located today. A development pamphlet produced around the time of the college's 75th anniversary explains that, "The founders of Suomi College had planned to get a stone from their homeland in Finland. It was to be the cornerstone in the first permanent building of Suomi. It would be a symbol of their native land, 'Suomi,' meaning 'Finland.' The stone never arrived. So the determined and steadfast founders of Suomi used a block of stone cut from the local Keweenaw quarries … There wasn't time—and perhaps not enough money—to properly engrave it. But Suomi had its first cornerstone."

13

SOUMI COLLEGE, HANCOCK, MICH.

E. G. KROPP, MILWAUKEE. MADE EXP. FOR GEO. H. NICHOLS

The first Suomi College building was designed by architect Charles Archibald Pearce in the Richardsonian Romanesque style. It is constructed of Jacobsville sandstone quarried at the Portage Entry of the Keweenaw waterway. The cost of the building was about $40,000: the stonework was $6,557, the woodwork, $10,037. (Finns in Michigan 396) Old Main was listed as a Michigan State Historic Site on February 12, 1959, and the National Register of Historic Places on January 13, 1972.

1900

Old Main was dedicated on Sunday, January 21. On the same cold, blustery day Suomi College students and faculty moved from their rented quarters into their new home.

There were few stone or brick buildings in Hancock at the time, so the new three-story sandstone structure was likely viewed as imposing and impressive. The upper two floors housed resident students, a house mother, and the president's quarters. Half of the first floor was a chapel, where services were held twice daily; business offices and classrooms occupied the remainder of the main level. The kitchen, dining room, and laundry were located in the basement.

Early images of the interior of Old Main are seen below and to the right.

The dining room.

CHAPTER TWO

1901-1910: A Difficult Childhood

Life was not easy in the early days of the college. One story tells of a Sunday evening when, returning from a trip to South Range and worried about the burdensome debt on Old Main, President Nikander asked the driver to stop and kneel with him as he prayed that God would bless Suomi College. (*Finns in Michigan* 399)

Future Suomi College president John Wargelin attended the college in these early years. He writes, "... On Saturdays the students scrubbed the floors of their rooms as well as the classroom floors, alternating between girls and boys. The rooms were heated by box stoves for which the boys carried the wood. The boys also kept the kitchen wood box filled by turns and thus earned the right during their service to a cup of coffee in the afternoon. There were no indoor toilets.

"If this seems primitive, we must add that this was the general standard at that time in Hancock. Life at the college in those early years was simple; and the cost of education was consequently low. Had it been higher, many of us would never have been able to get a college education." (*Faith of the Finns* 344)

John Wargelin.

Alex Leinonen (top), Isaac Sillberg (center), and Juho Jasberg.

Three pioneer laymen in particular were active in the early days of Suomi College. Alex Leinonen (1846-1902) was a friend from the start, serving as treasurer of the board until his death. "He was a man of conviction and gave his faithful service freely and joyfully." At Leinonen's funeral, Nikander described him as a faithful and modest friend of the school, "as steadfast in adversity as in prosperity." (*Golden Jubilee* 64-65)

Juho Heikki Jasberg (1861-1928) was "Nikander's right hand man and the college's first business manager. … He was the one who went himself or sent others to get money for Suomi. This task was not a 'bed of roses.' … He was an excellent speaker and a humorist. When he stepped onto the platform people were already smiling before he had a chance to say anything. … For years Mr. Jasberg worked together with Dr. Nikander in harmony … They complemented, strengthened, and helped each other." (*Golden Jubilee* 66) Jasberg married Nikander's sister, Wilhelmina, who had accompanied Nikander from Finland.

Isaac Sillberg (1857-1913) never missed a meeting of the college board, for which he was treasurer for 11 years. He was a generous contributor to the college. "The Sillberg's spacious and lovely home was always open to friends of Suomi College and Suomi Synod. … With his beautiful horse, 'Pekka', Mr. Sillberg met the visitors at the station and brought them home … During Christmas and Easter vacations many a student far away from his own, found here a friendly Christian home." (*Golden Jubilee* 66-67) For ten years, "Uncle Sillberg" and his wife, Elizabeth, provided a "home away from home" for Lydia Kangas-Ollila, one of Suomi's first graduates and later a teacher and dean.

In 1901 a frame building was built directly behind Old Main to house a gymnasium, music room, and meeting hall. Later, two-story additions were built at either end. In fall 1906 it became the home of the Commercial Department. The building served various purposes until 1940 when it was demolished upon completion of J. K. Nikander Hall.

Photos at right: Boys' and girls' physical education classes in the early 1900s.

Nikander was forty-seven years old when he married at the college in summer 1902. "If life at the young institution was clad with strict protocol, the president's marriage was certainly an enlivening factor. Somehow, boy met girl. In the annals of the college, the pattern of meeting one's spouse at Suomi College was established very early. Nikander set the tone." (The Way It Was 100-101)

1902

Suomi Synod and Suomi College co-founder K. L. Tolonen died suddenly on April 6.

In the same year, Nikander expressed his desire to resign as president of the college. When two possible replacements declined the position, Nikander agreed to continue.

For eight years, President Nikander resided in Old Main, living and dining with the students. One can only imagine the constant small, and not so small, crises he faced each day. In addition to his teaching and administrative duties, it is likely that he took on some of Old Main's upkeep and maintenance.

"On one occasion a person of feeble faith had spoken of the collapse of the school. To this Dr. Nikander had answered simply, 'If the College collapses, then I will be buried in its ruins.'" (*Golden Jubilee* 59-60)

Nikander, far right, with students in a Greek class.

1903-04 Suomi College faculty members (left to right): front row: J. K. Nikander, Alma Grandquist Haapanen, Lydia Silfven; back: D. W. Brandelle, J. Beck, L. Lund, K. V. Arminen, T. Wallenius.

1903

Five students completed the original seven-year course of study in spring 1903. However, they were asked to wait a year and graduate with the Class of 1904 the following spring. "During that year we could teach in the lower grades. We were to be paid $250.00 for this. We could also continue to study a few subjects during the year." (John Wargelin, *Faith of the Finns* 345-346)

A Preparatory Department was added to include the last two levels of grammar school. The only requirement for entrance was the ability to read a little Finnish. The department, which continued until 1923, served children nine years of age and up and those who were older but had little formal education.

Alma Granquist-Haapanen, who in 1903 traveled from Finland to teach at the college, writes, "What was Suomi like in those days? Old Main pulsated with life. There was not an empty room. Men and women lived in the same building, but they were not even allowed to use the same stairway to their rooms, except when some of the boys, favorites of Mrs. Lindgren, the good cook, carried washing to the attic. . . If at any other time the boys would have been seen on the girls' stairway, they probably would have landed in the 'putka.'

"What was the faculty like in 1903? I found their picture in the 'Suomi-Opiston Album' … Five of them were newcomers, three from Finland, two from here. I gazed at their faces. … Gone is Dr. J. K. Nikander, the beloved and respected founder and president of Suomi. Gone is the tall, slow-spoken science teacher, Maisteri K. V. Arminen, the absent-minded, pastor-philosopher, Johannes Beck, the blond, brilliant D. W. Brandelle, … the short, quick Maisteri Lauri Lund, who inspired everybody to sing so that the halls echoed with song, the reserved, melancholy Maisteri Toivo Wallenius, and the tiny blue-eyed, often blue-clad Miss Lydia Silfven." (*Golden Jubilee* 69-70)

A Suomi College picnic in 1905.

"We all worked hard both mentally and physically, but there were happy times, too . . . Frequently on a Saturday we would walk to Atlantic to visit friends, taking a shortcut by crossing Portage Lake by boat near the waterworks and returning the same day. Sometimes there were skiing trips, and we usually celebrated 'Laskiainen' sliding down a hill, even though sometimes the hill was only a pile of snow gathered in the yard over the fence of Dr. Nikander's home . . . We would sweep off a rink [for skating] on Portage Lake below the track, after the ice became safe." (Lydia Kangas-Ollila, *Golden Jubilee* 72)

1904

The combined graduating class of two women and seven men were awarded their diplomas on May 26, 1904. That fall, the seven men continued their studies in the Suomi College Theological Seminary.

Throughout its 54-year connection with Suomi College, the seminary never had a building of its own. Instead, it occupied at most one Old Main classroom and maintained a separate library. Several languages were taught, including Finnish, English, Latin, German, and Greek. Textbooks were chiefly in Finnish, with some in English and German.

The 1904 graduating class (left to right): back row: Lydia Kangas, Victor Koivumäki, Vilhelmiina (Minnie) Perttula, John Wargelin, Liisa Paavola; front: Alfred Haapanen, Matti Luttinen, Heikki Haapanen, Salomon Ilmonen. Not pictured is Pekka Keränen. The graduates ranged in age from 20 to 35 years old.

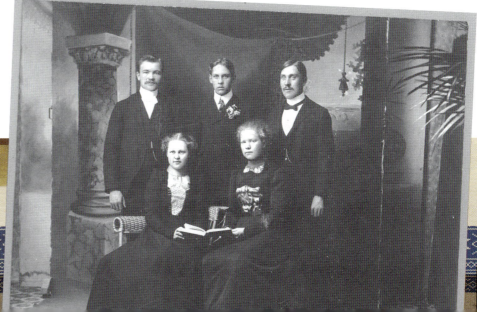

The Suomi College Class of 1903.

Suomi College teachers and students in 1906.

1906

Seven seminary students completed the two-year program in spring 1906 and were ordained. In 1908, one seminarian graduated, followed by five in 1912. In all, from 1906 to 1958, 119 men graduated from the seminary, with all entering the ministry of the Suomi Synod.

"The first (seminary) graduating class, one of the best, set the pace. Everyone in that class knew why he had come to Suomi. They knew what they wanted. They wanted a Christian education. They wanted to prepare themselves to be shepherds to thousands of Finns that had emigrated to this new land of freedom. They inspired and influenced the whole student body. They were an inspiration and help to me, a young, inexperienced teacher …" (Alma Granquist-Haapanen, *Golden Jubilee* 70)

John Wargelin wrote that, "After ten years my student days at Suomi College were ended. . . . I had come to the school at fourteen. (Many of the other students were from seven to ten years older). Now I was leaving as a man and an ordained minister." (*Faith of the Finns* 346)

By 1906 the academic program was reduced to a six-year format, which better accommodated entrance requirements for the University of Michigan. Classes three through six were the equivalent of high school grades nine through twelve. The first two classes were the adaptable, catch-all classes of the Preparatory Department.

Tuition in 1906 was $10 for the fall term and $15 dollars for the spring term, which was a little longer. For the Preparatory Department, student tuition was $7.00 and $8.00. Boarding students paid $2.50 per week. Books and other fees were about $8.00 for the year. (*Finns in North America* 99)

The 1906 seminary graduating class (left to right): front row: Victor Koivumäki, S. Ilmonen, John Wargelin, Matti Luttinen; back: Alfred Haapanen, Pekka Keränen, Jacob Mänttä.

President Nikander, a tireless fundraiser for the college, pointed out in 1906 that only about one-tenth of the annual amount needed to run the college was derived from tuition fees, which remained low in order to attract students. (*Faith of the Finns* 100) The balance came from voluntary gifts from individuals and congregations, as well as loans, special fund-raising campaigns, annual programs and festivals, personal pleas, and publication sales.

A local demand for trained office workers, especially those who could speak both Finnish and English, led to formation of the Commercial Department in fall 1906. Courses included bookkeeping, commercial law, arithmetic, penmanship, spelling, grammar, business correspondence, civil government, shorthand, and typewriting.

The Commercial Department, which awarded graduates a certificate of proficiency, became known for giving students a thorough foundation in business training, and it often had the largest college enrollment. It was led by O.L. Nordstrom until 1918, followed by Minnie Perttula-Maki for three years, then W. A. Lehto, who headed the department from 1920 to 1962. Under Lehto's leadership, the Commercial Department continued to grow and gained an enviable reputation.

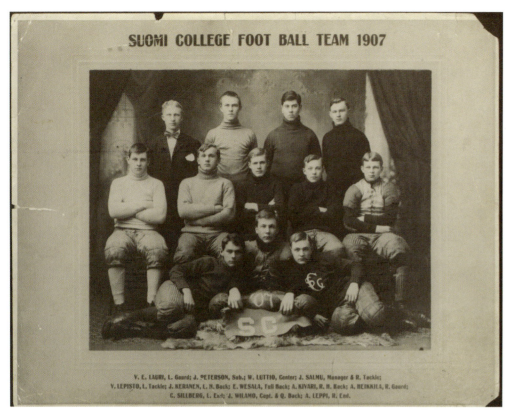

The 1907 Suomi College football team.

Raymond Wargelin in *The Way It Was* recalls that directly behind Old Main was another building, the Finnish Lutheran Book Concern, which was the synod's publishing house. A corridor leading from the front Quincy Street entrance of Old Main to the rear exit led, just outside, to the front entrance of the Book Concern building. "Students and faculty, as well as people with matters for the college business office and for the Book Concern, would frequently take advantage of the shortcut. … This became the basis for the comment: 'I have gone through Suomi College,' which made church members without much formal education equal to Suomi alumni. … The remark had a way of establishing a common basis between supporters and students." (99-100)

1907

From the beginning, training in piano, voice, and choral singing were part of the college's curriculum. The college became a music center for the church with instructors and students composing music for special occasions and student groups frequently performing public programs at churches and for community groups such as the Knights and Ladies of Kaleva. The 1908-09 college catalog lists music as a separate department, although a music certificate wasn't offered until 1927.

1910

By 1910, 243 students had attended the college, of which 139 were from Hancock and the Copper Country. Some 73% were from Michigan; 27% were from out of state, some from as far away as California and Massachusetts. (*Finns in Michigan* 398)

J. K. Nikander with his wife, Sanna Kristiina (Rajala), their sons, Toivo and Viljo, and their daughter, Aino. This portrait was probably taken around 1912. Alvaar Rautalahti wrote that "Dr. Nikander loved children and was a gentle and pious head of the family." (Golden Jubilee 61)

CHAPTER THREE

1911–1920: Challenging Social Issues and the Loss of Suomi's Pioneers

The years 1911 to 1920 were turbulent ones in the Copper Country. Widespread socialist anti-church sentiment and the 1913 Western Federation of Miners (WFM) strike defined much of the decade for the Suomi Synod.

Much of the socialist and labor movement energy was expended directly or indirectly at the church and Christianity. In Fitchburg, Mass., Astoria, Wash., and especially in Hancock, leftist Finnish American newspapers were numerous and among the first publications to serve anti-church attitudes. Books on socialism, economics, and social policies written from the point of view of materialism (which denies the existence of God) and the class struggle were also popular and widely distributed.

Holmio writes in *The History of the Finns in Michigan*, "It was strange that during the early phases of the labor struggle the church—and above all the Suomi Synod, which had its own clergy and publishing house—did not officially take a stand against materialism and for the Christian way of life, nor even clearly define its attitude toward the labor question." (282)

"Perhaps none put their necks on the line as clearly as the sainted genius, Pastor Viljami Rautanen, who defended the right to strike by copper mine workers in Calumet in 1913. It has been said that he taught in our seminary [Suomi College] without salary but was eased out because of his radical views at that time." (The Way It Was 65)

Not generally known was Rautanen's idiosyncrasy of always carrying a thermometer in his pocket. "When he visited a sick person, he always first stuck the thermometer in the person's mouth. His conversation was determined by whether or not the patient had a fever." (T.A. Kantonen, The Way It Was 95)

The manner of involvement by Suomi Synod clergy was left to the discretion of individual pastors. Some condemned socialism, while most remained neutral. Two synod pastors in particular, who were also Suomi College faculty members, were active in the discussions.

In his lectures at Suomi College and his articles in the synod publication *Kirkollinen Kalenteri* (Church Calendar), Pastor Iisakki Katajamaa was "unreservedly in favor of the workers' rights to improve their economic situation. At the same time, he severely criticized materialism and claimed that religion should not be allowed to enter into discussions about social problems." (*Finns in Michigan* 282)

Pastor Viljami Rautanen participated in the debate on the affirmative side. In articles published in "Amerikan Suometar" and in a short treatise, he expressed his views this way: "If the church doesn't include social problems in its program and strive for their solution, others will do so, and what is even worse, they may do so in the wrong spirit or use a one-sided approach. … Insofar as possible, the church should become more than ever involved in social problems. Such are, for example, the care of the needy, labor movements, and trade unions." (*Finns in Michigan* 282-283)

The WFM strike was abandoned in April 1914 with some of the miners' demands met. In the 1920s, anti-church sentiments began to subside.

Left: The 1914-15 Suomi College girls' basketball team.

Below: The 1914-15 Suomi College boys' basketball team. "The boys' team got started quite late in the season because ... we were unable to get a hall for practice ... [but we] played with good spirit, winning many of the hard games. ... The girls' team ... had only two opportunities to show us their grit." (1915 Suomite 47)

1918

Synod and college leaders instituted a synod-wide fundraising campaign, "Suomi College Week," which, in just two years, made it possible to retire the debt on Old Main. Yet the college was still compelled to survive day-to-day as it seemed impossible to raise sufficient funds for expansion.

John Wargelin notes in his 1923 master's degree thesis that in 1921, when the college became free of debt, there was talk of moving Suomi to a more central location and that a number of cities expressed interest to the college board, including Duluth, Minnesota, and Painesville, Ohio.

"But ... it does not appear probable that [the college] will be moved away from Hancock," Wargelin writes. "The city has always shown great interest in the school, and when the question of a new location came up, the Chamber of Commerce of Hancock appointed a committee to ... find out what could be done to keep the school in its present location. This only shows that Suomi College has made friends in wide sections of our country." (*Americanization of the Finns* 111-112)

SUOMI COLLEGE BASKET BALL TEAM
1914-1915.

A collage of student life from the 1913-14 Suomi College yearbook.

The Commercial Department Class of 1915.

1919

J. K. Nikander, who had arrived in Hancock on January 5, 35 years earlier, died January 13, 1919, two days after suffering a stroke, leaving Suomi College as his permanent memorial. The student body numbered 165 that year, a number not surpassed until 1946 when his son, V. K. Nikander, was president of the college.

"To the memory of the beloved president of Suomi College since its foundation in 1896, Dr. Juho Kustaa Nikander, whose teachings and counsels are living within us, we the students of 1919, gratefully dedicate this volume." (Suomi yearbook, 1919)

Like all the yearbooks published by Suomi College students from 1915 to 1932, the 1918-19 edition contained both Finnish and English language text. The yearbooks reveal a vivid portrait of the life of the college. Essays, poems, short fiction, and original music scores join line drawings, individual and group photos, and nicknames and "classifications" of graduating seniors, such as the "most dignified lady" and "the gayest laughter."

A September 28 entry on the 1918-19 yearbook calendar of activities reads, "Vendla and Siiri got a ride in the Suomi Auto." On November 8, "Six girls were locked out after 10:00 p.m.," and on November 11, world peace was declared. On January 11, "Dr. Nikander was paralyzed," on January 19, "Sad news – Dr. Nikander died," and "Dr. Nikander's funeral" on January 17.

The floral arrangements surrounding Nikander's coffin.

John Wargelin.

"His quiet persistence in the face of obstacles, his calm conviction, self-effacing devotion to his task, and his vision qualified him for the position of leader of the school," writes Edward J. Isaac of Nikander in the 1946 *Golden Jubilee* publication. "His humble trust in divine guidance and conviction that the call of the College was from God was a source of inspiration and strength to many others." (24-25)

When Nikander became president of the Suomi Synod in 1890, there were four pastors and nine congregations. In 1919 the synod had 44 pastors and 154 congregations.

"Dr. Nikander's greatest work as a Church leader was accomplished, after all, through his labors in Suomi College and Theological Seminary," writes Raymond Wargelin. "His work here meant that educated people could assume the leadership in the immigrant Finnish community." (*Faith of the Finns* 332)

Nikander's death marked the end of Suomi's "pioneer" period. K. L. Tolonen had died in 1902, J. W. Eloheimo in 1913, and J. J. Hoikka in 1917.

A few weeks before his death, Nikander had corresponded with Wargelin about the vacant position as manager of the college. "On the very day of his death I received a postcard from him stating that he approved my being called to that position," Wargelin writes in *The Faith of the Finns*. (346)

At the next meeting of the board of directors, Wargelin was appointed manager and elected president *pro tem*. Later that spring, Wargelin's election as president was made permanent. He served in this dual capacity until his resignation in June 1927, returning as president from 1930 to 1937.

Faculty members in the early 1920s included (clockwise from lower left): Dr. Alfred Haapanen, Rev. Vihtori Koivumäki, Rev. Victor Kuusisto, and Minnie Perttula-Maki.

Seminary faculty members in 1914 or 1915 (left to right): John Saarinen, Niilo Karhonen, and Otto Maki.

1920

The year 1920 was the first in which most college classes were taught in English, yet Finnish traditions were carefully guarded and the religious life of the college fostered.

The Preparatory Department/Academy became an accredited high school in the state of Michigan in 1920, which made it possible for graduates to continue their educations at a larger number of colleges and universities. The Academy was discontinued in 1932 for a number of reasons, including a growing number of public high schools in even the smallest communities.

By 1920, the Commercial Department claimed as much as sixty-five percent of total college enrollment. At the end of each school year, jobs for Suomi College Commercial Department graduates were virtually guaranteed.

CHAPTER FOUR

1921-1930: Americanization

A flag-raising ceremony in 1923.

"At this stage of Suomi's development … the college rapidly lost its 'immigrant' character and became more and more typically American," writes V. J. Nikander of the 1920s. "The complexion of the student body changed. In place of the Finnish-born immigrants came their children, the American-born second generation which had its entire grade and secondary school education in the United States." (*Golden Jubilee* 43-44)

Right: The 1926 Suomi College Choir during a summer session at the American Academy in Rome, Italy. Music director Martti Nisonen is seated in the center of the front row.

Handwritten on the reverse of this 1939 photo is, "The Finnish volunteers from the Copper Country are singing 'Over There,' World War ditty, at the piano in their drill hall with Prof. Martti Nisonen, director of music at Suomi College, at the keys. They are scheduled to leave in the middle of March [to fight in Finland's Winter War]. Prof. Nisonen, who fought with Mannerheim to establish Finland as a republic, is the leader of the volunteer movement. His son accompanied a batch of volunteers which left earlier, & is now fighting in Finland."

1922

Martti Nisonen became head of the Music Department in 1922, and he did much to stimulate the musical life of the college. He originated a well-received four-week summer music course in 1925, which continued annually for more than two decades. In 1927, the college began to grant a special music certificate after two years of study. Nisonen also continued his predecessors' work in arranging semi-annual concerts, which were important events in the life of the college for several decades.

Nisonen "had the profile and bushy hair of a maestro. His musical ability and eccentricity became memorable. … Nisonen as a pianist was a guaranteed spectacle. … usually a few keys were dislodged by [his] powerful playing. … There was always something dramatic about Nisonen's musical events." (*The Way It Was* 102)

Old Main in the 1920s.

Suomi College

Minnie Perttula-Maki was interim president from 1922 to 1923 while President John Wargelin completed his master's degree at University of Michigan. She is the only woman to date to serve as president of the college. Perttula-Maki was also active in the temperance movement and the Suomi Synod. She did not draw attention to her unique and important status as a leader of the college, according to her stepdaughter, Gertrude Johnson. Johnson described her stepmother, who died in 1957 at age 77, as warm and friendly, energetic, committed to community service, and well read. "She was a great lady." (March 1987 Bridge 3)

For many years, the ambition of the college administration was that a four-year college would become a reality. Many difficulties, primarily financial, hindered this desire, but in 1922 a committee concluded that a Junior College was within reach.

"The beginning of the Junior College was a studied and deliberate move … to find a place for Suomi in the American educational scheme and particularly in higher education. The Junior College movement in the United States was growing rapidly. …" (V. K. Nikander, *Golden Jubilee* 44)

1923

In fall 1923 the Junior College enrolled its first class of four students. The seminary course was increased from two to three years, and those wishing to enter the seminary were now required to graduate from the Junior College. First-year Junior College courses included English Rhetoric, U.S. History, Psychology, Philosophy, Christianity, and Chemistry; second-year courses were English Literature, Greek or German, Christianity, Biology, and Education.

Junior College growth was slow. Explanations included lack of confidence in the school, fear that one must know the Finnish language, too strong a religious emphasis, and competition from larger, more established colleges.

For the Junior College to succeed, new equipment and facilities and an endowment were needed. In 1930, after much discussion among board members and administration, a capital campaign was undertaken. The goal of $300,000 was not reached, but pledges of over $82,000 were made, with $47,000 of that in cash by 1935. With the funds, library holdings were increased, new laboratory equipment was purchased, and the nucleus of an endowment was established. It's likely that the funds also helped the college survive the Great Depression.

As a result of improvements to the library and laboratory, and more stringent requirements for faculty, in 1931 the Junior College was accredited by the University of Michigan.

1924

The college began offering Saturday and evening classes in English, political science, shorthand, and Swedish for those who could not attend weekday classes. The program enjoyed modest success.

A Commercial Department typewriting class in the 1920s. Minnie Perttula-Maki is standing at the back of the class.

Finnish artist Akseli Gallen-Kallela (1865-1931) visited the college in February 1924 as a guest of the synod. Later, he gave to the college these two drawings and additional pieces of his artwork.

1926

In spring 1926, 31 students graduated from the Academy, 20 from the Commercial Department. That fall five students enrolled in the Junior College. The 1926 *Suomian* says of the Junior College, "Comparatively young in years, and rather small in size is [the Junior College] at Suomi College. But it is large, indeed, in zeal, activity and earnestness. … The Junior College Department seeks to meet a two-fold call: the call of the student for a less expensive educational system, and the call of our large universities for help in caring for the undergraduate department." (1926 *Suomian* 29)

The 1927 men's forensics team. An approximate translation of the words below the photo: "Learning to speak to others as well as [among] ourselves."

The 1926–27 girls' basketball team. "Following the custom of former years the girls of Suomi College organized a Basketball team, but due to the new Legislation that High School girls are not to be permitted to play Basketball, they were unable to get many games scheduled." (1927 *Suomian* 14)

1927

In 1927 Suomi's men's basketball team "plunged into hitherto unexplored fields and entered the district tournament" at Michigan Technological University. "Enthusiasm prevailed throughout the whole college. ... The real thrill came that evening when the team ... stepped up to receive the cup for the Class championship." (1927 Suomian 43)

In spring 1927 President John Wargelin resigned in response to opposition by some synod leaders to the "Americanization" of the college. "The agitation was apparently caused by some necessary changes made at the college, and particularly because I had written a book entitled, 'The Americanization of the Finns,'" Wargelin writes. "This book was written as a thesis for my Master's Degree at the University of Michigan. … some … thought the purpose of the book was to hasten the Americanization of the Finns. This was not the intent. …" (*Faith of the Finns* 346-347)

Among John Wargelin's first-term achievements were instituting English as the language of instruction in most subjects; retiring $20,000 of the Old Main debt through a synod-wide "Suomi College Week" fundraising campaign begun in 1918; and accreditation of the Academic Department by the University of Michigan. Special guests at the college's 25th anniversary celebration included the bishop of the Church of Finland, the president of the United Lutheran Church in America, and representatives from a number of Lutheran colleges.

Pastor Antti Lepisto succeeded Wargelin as president, serving until 1930 when Wargelin was persuaded to return. Wargelin again resigned as president in 1937, continuing on the theological faculty until May 1939.

In *Faith of the Finns* Wargelin recalls that, "The Board of Directors invited me back to Suomi College. I declined. They turned to me a second time, and again I declined. . . . the Board of Directors of the college sent a committee of three men to see me personally . . . In this last appeal the committee said to me, 'If you have any love for Suomi College, she needs you now.' I returned to Suomi College. . . ." (347-348)

Antti Lepisto.

President Lepisto with students in a Parish Workers class. A Bible institute to train church lay workers was begun by Lepisto in 1928. It failed to find a response and was discontinued after two years.

Like other schools of its kind, Suomi College was primarily dedicated to the cause of Christian education. "What, then, are its aims and objectives?" John Wargelin asks in the 1946 *Golden Jubilee* publication. Wargelin often illustrated the college's objectives using each of the letters S-U-O-M-I to stand for an ideal. (29)

S — *Suomi* indicates Finnish. It is a reminder of the founders of the school.

U — *Uskonto*, religion. This points to its Christian function.

O — *Oppilaitos*, school. It is an institution of higher learning.

M — *Miehuus*, 'virtutis,' manliness. It aims to develop the whole person, body, mind, and spirit without overemphasis upon any of them.

I — *Isänmaallisuus*, patriotism. It aims to train its students to become good citizens.

Lepisto earned his bachelor of arts degree at the University of Chicago and was ordained in 1921. Here he leads a class in Old Main.

1930

The Suomi College "Sampo Society," an honor society, was established by faculty in spring 1930. Considered for membership were the most outstanding and active students. The "sampo" is a magic mill from the Finnish epic, *The Kalevala*. It signifies happiness and common good; it is a product of skill, knowledge, and power; and it supplies the needs of those who possess it.

 The original Sampo Society insignia has a small "s" for Suomi and a larger "S" for the greater Suomi. Two hands clasped together in friendship and good cause can also be seen. Kosti Erlund ('31), admitted to the Sampo Society in 1930, writes of society honorees that, "It is our honorable duty, fellow members, to keep the Greater Suomi College as our aim and to work for it, thus trying to repay the great blessings we have received from our Alma Mater."

Photos at left: Class of 1931 graduates (from the top) Alice Aula, William Bilto, Dorothy Collins, Elvi Donner, and Kosti Erlund.

The Academy Department Class of 1932 was the last. Graduates were Eleanor Elm, Hazel Nelson, Sylvia Wargelin, John Hattula, and John Koivisto.

A five-mile hike to College Point, or "Opistonniemi," was a fall tradition in the early years of the college. Aino I. Nikander, the daughter of J. K. Nikander, recalls that "In the fall, after school got under way … an excursion would be arranged for the whole student body, as well as the teachers … the road wound along beautiful lakeshore … and gay laughter rang on the Canal Road … it finally came into view, a lovely spot."

First, the students would build a fire in the stove of a little cabin and make coffee. Photos were taken, sandwiches eaten, and games played, including one on the road called "Last Couple Out," which required "a fleet bit of footwork. …"

"This type of activity was instrumental in breaking down barriers of reserve among many of the students … Firm bonds of friendship were formed … and many a romantic attachment later led to the altar." (*Golden Jubilee* 76-77)

Noted on the back of this spring 1929 photo were the hometowns of the pictured students. They hailed from near and far: DeKalb, Ill., Hurley, Wis., Sault Ste. Marie, Canada, and, in Michigan, Agate, Ahmeek, Atlantic Mine, Boston, Chassell, Crystal Falls, Eben, Hancock, Houghton, Iron Mountain, L'Anse, Mohawk, Negaunee, Nisula, Sault Ste. Marie, Toivola, Trout Creek, and Wainola.

CHAPTER FIVE

1931-1940: Building Character and the Depression Years

The Great Depression, which began in the early 1930s and lasted until the start of WWII, affected everyone and Suomi College was no exception. Money was scarce, enrollment fell, and those who supported the college financially had less ability to do so. But by the end of the decade, the nation and the college had survived. Suomi had even begun construction of a new building. The institution's collective sisu had triumphed again.

Kosti Arho, Finnish instructor from 1922 to 1949, as well as college librarian, longtime treasurer of the synod, and editor of "Amerikan Suometar" was "meticulous in spotting all the wrong case endings (there are fifteen of them) . . .[but] he was loaded with numerous other responsibilities, chief of which was preparing the Finnish language bulletins for the press. As a result, whenever anyone would meet him on the campus, he had his eyes riveted upon the papers he was correcting, completely oblivious to people. It was always a wonder how he could do this and not run into a door or some person." (*The Way It Was* 104-105)

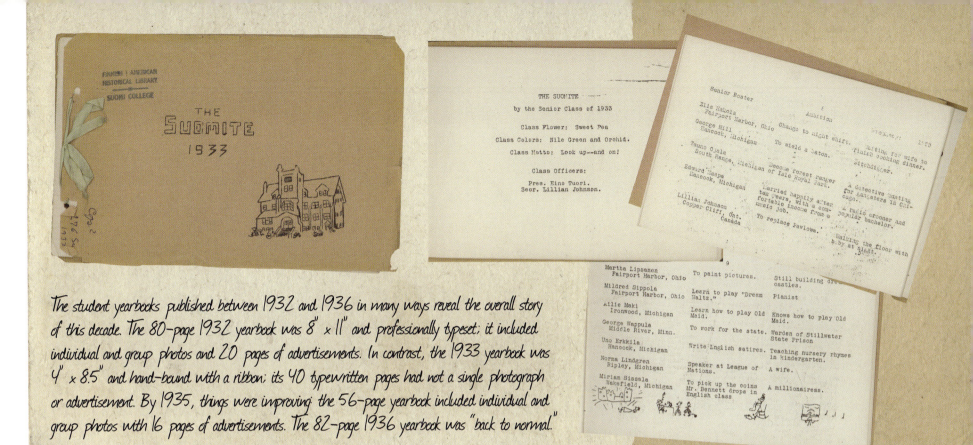

The student yearbooks published between 1932 and 1936 in many ways reveal the overall story of this decade. The 80-page 1932 yearbook was 8" x 11" and professionally typeset; it included individual and group photos and 20 pages of advertisements. In contrast, the 1933 yearbook was 4" x 8.5" and hand-bound with a ribbon; its 40 typewritten pages had not a single photograph or advertisement. By 1935, things were improving: the 56-page yearbook included individual and group photos with 16 pages of advertisements. The 82-page 1936 yearbook was "back to normal."

1932

On the topic, "Greater Suomi," the theme of the 1932 college yearbook, President John Wargelin writes, "Suomi College has endeared itself to a host of friends through its thirty-six years of service. … [it] is a small institution, but there are those who love it. … there are certain things which a small college does not need to yield to any school, and that is in molding character."

1930s Commercial graduate Elma Kyrm writes of the college in 1946 that she "wanted to prepare for a career, so that I would be able to support myself, and Suomi College gave me that training. … Suomi College stressed the building of good character. … Upon leaving a secretarial position, my 'boss' came to me and asked, 'Do you know why this position was given to you? … I answered in the negative … 'It was your smile. As you stepped into the consultation room, you bowed slightly and greeted us with a pleasant smile.' I almost gasped, for I did not know I had smiled and to this day cannot recall it, but I do know that it gave me a job at a time when thousands were knocking at doors, pleading for work. … I attribute it to my Alma Mater for giving me a sound preparation, plus a personality training." (*Golden Jubilee* 78-79)

The year 1932 marked the end of the Academy Department, which was no longer needed as accredited public high schools now served virtually all communities, large and small. In its more than three decades, the Academy awarded diplomas to about 175 graduates, and hundreds of others received instruction in the department.

In 1932 the Junior College was approved by University of Michigan examiners, so that students transferring from Suomi to other schools in Michigan would suffer no loss of credits. The colleges of the United Lutheran Church in America also agreed, in general, to accept Suomi transfer credits in full.

Enrollment in the Junior College increased, even during the Depression. In 1933 the Board set up a program of twelve stipends a year that canceled freshman year tuition, a program that continued for many years. And to reduce financial pressures on the school, in 1932 the teachers consented to a five to ten percent reduction in their salaries, and another ten percent reduction in 1933; these remained in force for about five years. (*Finns in North America* 110)

The Commercial Department Class of 1931. Waino "Pop" Lehto, principal of the Commercial Department, is seated in the center of the front row. Lehto's tenure with Suomi as instructor and dean spanned more than 40 years, from 1920 to 1962.

Suomi College faculty in 1931 (left to right): front row: Elizabeth Mitchell, Sanna Nikander (Dean of Girls), John Wargelin (President), Alma Van Slyke, Aino Nikander; back: Waino A. Lehto (Principal of the Commercial Dept.), Ilmari Tammisto, Martti Nisonen (Director of Music), Edward Isaac (Business Manager), Kosti Arho, C. L. Vigness.

Educated in Finland, Tammisto was an excellent teacher and respected by his seminary students, but he always looked very youthful. During fall registration in 1930, he was asked by a student what courses he was taking. "Tammisto, being a teacher of the European school, soon let the enquiring student know who he was."
(The Way it Was 105-106)

In the early days of the college, Jasberg had established a college museum, but Rev. Ilmari Tammisto was the first to turn his attention to the college's collection of Finnish American publications. A professor of systematic theology and Christianity from 1930 to 1937, Tammisto began to organize the materials as an archives collection, but a lack of funds and trained personnel hindered any real progress. When Tammisto returned to Finland in 1937 the matter was shelved until the 1945-46 academic year when Dr. John Kolehmainen, professor of history on leave from Heidelberg College, conducted research at the college and began to catalogue the material at hand and collect more. But the archive collection still had no permanent home.

In 1932 the college and seminary arranged a week-long pastors' institute, which continued annually in the spring semester for about 15 years. A well-known theologian would be the principal lecturer, assisted by seminary instructors and synod pastors.

The 1931 Junior College graduating class included future Suomi College director of music Art Hill. Hill is second from the right in the back row.

A student life collage from the 1934 yearbook.

1933

A senior roster in the 1933 college yearbook illustrates the hopes—and the realities—of the Depression years and reveals much about the students' worries for the future … as well as their sense of humor. Below is this roster, which includes each student's name, hometown, ambition, and prophesy of where they see themselves in 20 years.

Elis Hakola; Fairport Harbor, Ohio; change to night shift; waiting for wife to finish cooking dinner.

George Hill; Hancock, Mich.; to wield a baton; ditch digger.

Tauno Ojala; South Range, Mich.; become a Forest Ranger of Isle Royal Park; a detective hunting for gangsters in Chicago.

Martha Lipsanen; Fairport Harbor, Ohio; to paint pictures; still building dream castles.

Norma Lindgren; Ripley, Mich.; speaker at the League of Nations; a wife.

Miriam Sissala; Wakefield, Mich.; to pick up the coins Mr. Bennett drops in English class; a millionairess.

Arnold Stadius; Astoria, Ore.; to be an archaeologist; kindergarten teacher.

Jack Starberg; Palo, Minn.; head of Lacta Separator Company, Finland; milking cows on a farm in Minnesota.

Melvin Lindgren; Ripley, Mich.; to be a Captain of Industry; a lumber jack.

Mayme Saari; Wakefield, Mich.; to be an efficient secretary; washerwoman.

1934

In spring 1934, 22 graduated from the Junior College, 23 from the Commercial Department, and one completed the Music Department certificate: the "solemn, solid and good-hearted" George "Gregory" Hill of Hancock. An advertisement in that yearbook indicates that annual tuition was, for the Junior College, $85; Commercial Department, $80; Music Department, $70; and Theological Seminary, $60.

The 1934 yearbook begins, "Despite the difficulties that we realized would be before us, in issuing this annual, we, the Class of 1934, were determined to have some sort of a memory of our two profitable years at Suomi. Because of financial difficulties, our yearbook must be in an abbreviated form …" (4)

The science laboratory in 1931.

"The youth of today finds himself in a different kind of a world than faced the youth of a previous age," writes John Wargelin. "The world is in the midst of a great transition. … Life has become complex in the extreme. … Your duty will be to face the problems of life with an enlightened judgment and sympathetic appreciation of the cultural and spiritual heritage of the past." (1934 *Suomian* 33-34)

In fall 1934 just 28 students were enrolled, nine of them in the seminary. Their yearbook states that they "entered meekly, eager to obtain the knowledge which we had so long desired." (1934 *Suomian* 16)

The Suomi College Class of 1934.

1936

"Many interesting comparisons could be made between Suomi College of 1896 and that of 1936," writes John Wargelin in the 1936 yearbook. Of the students enrolling in Suomi's first year, about 95 percent were born in Finland, while in 1936 the opposite was true, as about 98 percent of the Finnish students were American-born.

Wargelin also notes changes in the ethnic and religious composition of the student body. Until 1913 all Suomi students were of Finnish extraction, and until 1930 occasionally there were one or two non-Finnish speaking students. But with the reorganization of the Junior College in 1930 the student body increasingly included students of many ethnicities and religious affiliations. The students enrolled in 1935-36 identified affiliation with the following denominations: 80 Lutherans, 16 Roman Catholics, 6 Methodists, 4 Presbyterians, 2 Congregationalists, and one each, Baptist, Greek Orthodox, and Jewish. (1936 *Suomian* 40-41)

Suomi College and Theological Seminary

invites students to the following four departments:

JUNIOR COLLEGE	Tuition $85.00 per year,
COMMERCIAL DEPARTMENT	„ 80.00 „ „
MUSIC DEPARTMENT	„ 70.00 „ „
THEOLOGICAL SEMINARY	„ 60.00 „ „

Registration fee ..$2.50, paid only once.
Library fee ......$2.00, per semester.

Faculty consists of men and women who have completed graduate work in several outstanding universities of America and Europe.

Diploma relations have been established with various other colleges and universities.

FALL TERM opens Tuesday, September 3, 1935.

Bulletin will be sent free of charge on request.

JOHN WARGELIN, *President.*

A Suomi College advertisement in the 1935 yearbook.

The Aeolus Society in 1936.

The seminary class of 1936 included future college president Raymond Wargelin, back row, center. In 1936, 84% of all Suomi Synod ministers were graduates of the Suomi Theological Seminary.

A number of Suomi College student organizations endured for many decades. They included Suomalainen Konventti, the oldest student group, established in 1901, whose purpose was preserving Finnish culture. The Philomathic Society promoted culture and the development of self-expression in the English language. Its programs included dramatizations and readings of prose and poetry. The Aeolus Society promoted the interests of music and culture. Regular meetings featured speakers, discussion, and musical performances. Others were the boys' and girls' Athletic Associations, the Suomi College Choir, the Luther League, which replaced the Bible Society in 1934, and the Sampo Honor Society.

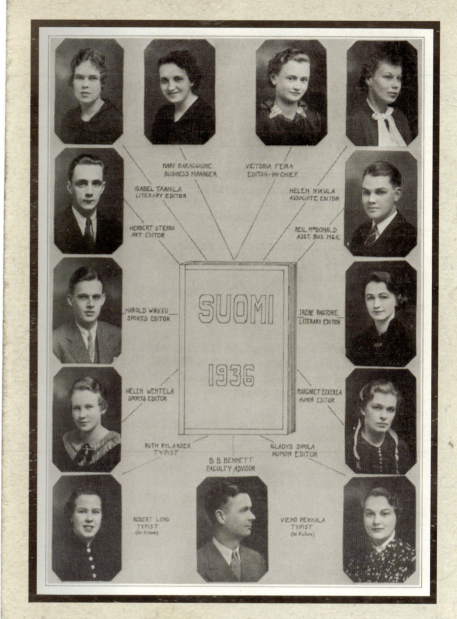

The members of the 1936 Suomian yearbook staff were: editor-in-chief Victoria Feira; business manager Mary Baraggione and assistant business manager Neil McDonald; associate editor Helen Nikula; literary editors Irene Pastore and Isabel Taanila; humor editors Margaret Eckerea and Gladys Sipola; sports editors Helen Wentela and Harold Wirkku; art editor Herbert Stierna; typists Vieno Pekkala, Robert Long, and Ruth Rylander; and faculty advisor B. B. Bennett.

1937

Wargelin asked to be relieved of his responsibilities as president of Suomi College, although he continued as an instructor in the seminary. Dr. Viljo K. Nikander, the son of Suomi College founder J. K. Nikander, succeeded him, holding the office for 10 years. Born in 1903, V.K. Nikander was a graduate of the academy and the seminary. He earned a B.S. degree from Carthage College, an M.A. from the University of Chicago, and a Ph.D. from Harvard University.

V. K. Nikander in the 1920s and 1940s.

Suomi College students found many ways earn the cost of tuition. One of them was to teach for the *keskäkoulu* (summer school), which began in 1911 and was co-sponsored by the Evangelical and Apostolic Lutheran churches.

Bertha (Simi) Collar, a 1937 graduate, taught the three-week summer schools for eight summers, in Nisula, Kyro-Pelkie, Elo, and Covington, Michigan. Her pay was $20.00 and room and board at a private home. "Pop, Maisteri Waino Lehto, my economics professor at Suomi, conducted a brief training session in the spring of 1936 for [interested Suomi College students]," she recalls in *The Way It Was*. Bertha also met with the summer school committee of "six to eight very devout gentlemen from both churches," writing that they "heartily approved of the curriculum [she had developed] … They were very gracious to an 18-year-old, calling me '*Neiti* (Miss) Simi this, and *Neiti* that.'" (143-145)

Summer school classes were taught in Finnish until the early 1940s. Subjects included Bible history and the catechism, as well as study of the Finnish language. Books used were the *Aapinen* (ABCs), *Katekismus* (catechism), *Raamatun Historia* (Bible history), *Lukukirja* (number reader), and the *Pyhäkoulun Laulukirja* (Sunday School songbook).

Rev. Rudolph Kemppainen, 1955 seminary graduate, recalls in *The Way It Was* that summer school was a highlight of the typically uneventful summer in Salo, a rural farming community northeast of Hancock in which he was born and raised. "Summer school had a profound impact on my life," Kemppainen writes, recalling that, "At the veritable point of tears, I was compelled to learn and practice the *Aapinen*. Little did I realize then that I was learning a language that I would preach and teach for the next 35 years of my life as a bilingual pastor of the church." (59)

1938

In 1938 a twelve-week campaign to fund a new building was undertaken by President Nikander, who travelled widely to promote it. Pledges of over $97,000 were received, exceeding the $75,000 goal. More than half of the pledges came from Copper Country residents and over $80,000 from friends of the college in the Midwest.

Students and faculty in 1938.

1939

The "New Building," later named J. K. Nikander Hall, was planned by architect Eliel Sarinen and his son-in-law, architect J. R. F. Swanson. The land on which it was built was purchased from the defunct Hancock Mining Company and covered about 60 acres. The architects also laid out a long-range building plan for the college.

"It is a pleasure to see the bricklayers lay brick upon brick, to watch the carpenters fit the windows and stairs, to smell the sweet aroma of the new lumber, and to hear one's voice echo through the halls," students write in the first issue of *Inklings*, in October 1939. (2)

In anticipation of the new building, changes were made to Old Main to house the Commercial Department and the seminary classrooms were relocated to the former Commercial building. The college now had a physical plant that could serve at least 150 students.

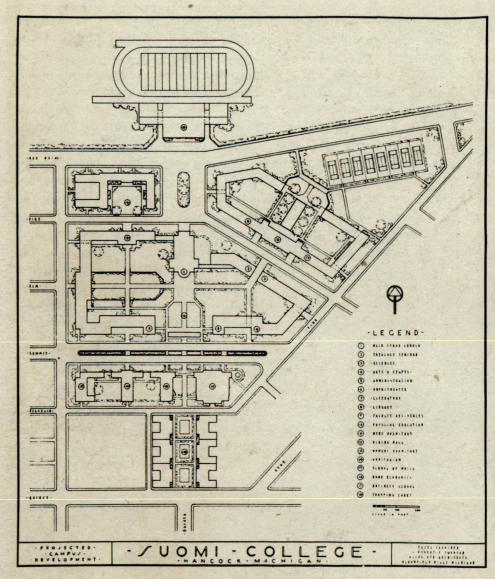

NEW CAMPUS PLAN
Architects: Eliel Saarinen, J. R. F. Swanson

A "New Campus Plan" designed in 1939 by architects Eliel Sarinen and J. R. F. Swanson.

The groundbreaking for Nikander Hall was on May 5, 1939, and the cornerstone was laid on June 13. "The City of Hancock cooperated splendidly in making possible the plans of the architect by extending a street through the property, thus allowing access to the building from both Summit and Franklin Streets." (Golden Jubilee 21)

J. K. Nikander Hall
June 13, 1939

Alfred A. Haapanen, a graduate of the first seminary class in 1906, led fundraising campaigns for the college between 1929 and 1950. President of the Suomi Synod from 1922 to 1950, Haapanen was a leader in the synod's and the college's transition from Finnish to English. "Without a doubt, he was the 'public relations man' with the longest record the college has ever had," writes Raymond Wargelin in The Faith of the Finns. (339)

INKLINGS

Vol. 1 — No. 1   Suomi College, Hancock, Michigan — October, 1939   Five Cents

Board Convenes At College

The board of directors of Suomi College held its regular fall meeting on Tuesday, September 26, and elected the following officers for the ensuing year.

Chairman — Rev. M. Luttinen

First Day of School Is Day of Eager Anticipation

A group of enthusiastic and seemingly promising students and capable teachers gathered at the Finnish Evangelical Lutheran Church on Tuesday morning, September 12, 1939, to attend the service which was to start a new school year at Suomi

Suomi Students Come From All Parts of United States

Eight states and Canada have representatives at Suomi College this year. From New Castle, Pennsylvania, comes Arvo Niskanen, Esther Halttunen, and Jennie Marttala. Students from Ohio are Bernhard Hillila of

New Instructors Are Selected

Mr. Conley R. Addington, newly appointed instructor of Business Administration in the Junior College and assistant in commercial studies, is a native of Virginia. He received his B.S. degree from William and Mary College and his M.B.A. degree in

---

Inklings, a student newspaper begun in 1939 and published several times a year until December 1971, included news of campus activities, student clubs and sports, inspirational quotes from the likes of Emerson, Thoreau, and Twain, alumni news, faculty bios, book reviews, cartoons and jokes, advice columns, and editorials. Typically a four- to eight-page tabloid, Inklings was distributed free on campus and mailed nationwide to alumni and friends.

During the 1930s, students in the Junior College began a one-week freshman initiation which took place early in the fall semester. "On the whole the sophs were quite successful in making the freshies toe the line," students write in the October 1939 issue of *Inklings*. "Drastic penalties" were planned for those who deviated from the sophomore law. (4)

The fall 1939 sophomore "rules," evidently formulated anew each fall, included: Boys must wear green neckties and tie clasps at all times while at the college; Freshman ladies must wear their hair parted in the middle, with a green bow on either side. The boys must do the same, but may omit the bows; Sweaters must be worn inside out; On or before October 13, each freshman must bring a nice red apple for the sophomores' food supply; When meeting sophomores on the sidewalk, freshmen are to stand at attention on the street until the sophomores have passed; Don't call sophomores by nicknames or first names. They must be addressed as Mr. and Miss; and so on. (May 1939 *Inklings* 4)

1940

The "New Building" (later named Nikander Hall) was completed and occupied in December 1939 and dedicated June 15, 1940, in conjunction with the 50th anniversary of the Suomi Synod, a six-day event attended by as many as 3,000 people. The four levels of the new building, constructed by general contractor Herman Gundlach, included a combined gymnasium and auditorium, biology and chemistry labs, classrooms and offices, a music room, a dining hall, a library, and a campus heating plant. The new building, without equipment, cost $90,000, the total project, $125,000. In November 1942 a Victory Drive initiated by the synod and carried out by Suomi alumni raised $14,500 toward the cost of the building and fixtures, but considerable debt remained for many years.

Having survived the Great Depression, Suomi College students, faculty, staff, board members, and friends surely looked forward to the new decade with hope. That hope may have also been tempered with apprehension as the United States witnessed the start of another war in Europe.

CHAPTER SIX

1941–1950: The War Years, Resurgence, and a Celebration

The decade of the 1940s was marked by struggle as the school endured low enrollment and restricted funding. But there were celebrations as well, including the end of World War II and the school's 50th anniversary. As it had so many times, Suomi not only prevailed, but grew stronger.

1941

Student enrollment began to drop steadily following the United States' entrance into World War II in December 1941. College programs were curtailed as the institution marked time through the war years. It became necessary to draw on the endowment fund and borrow to cover regular expenses.

"The Suomi College of the early 1940s had become a fairly typical church-related institution in most ways, but Finnish still had a vibrant roll to play," writes David Halkola in *The Way It Was*. "Most of the residential students came from an environment that had retained the language; the meetings of the 'Konventti Club' did not lack participants because Finnish was spoken. … All those expecting to be ordained were expected to learn or perfect the use of the language. Ironically, these young men were among the last of that category; a few years later, after World War II, the inevitable shift had become apparent, even though it was resisted in a sort of rear-guard action almost to the very end of the Suomi Synod as an independent entity." (173)

The Class of 1941.

An annual Religious Emphasis Week was begun at the college in 1941 and it continued for more than two decades. Held during the spring semester, the event was intended to "awaken and deepen" students' spiritual life. Activities included guest speakers and opportunities for students to consult campus and community spiritual leaders about spiritual matters and personal problems.

Students and faculty in fall 1942.

1942

In 1942 Nikander instituted the sale of defense stamps on campus, each month appointing a team of student "vendors." Campus scrap drives were organized, and in November 1944 a large number of gifts were received at a "shower" hosted on campus to benefit Finnish war orphans.

Junior College course offerings were curtailed during the war, and in 1943 all the faculty members, except the seminary instructors, were working on a part-time basis. Through this extreme economy, during these years the college was able to reduce the building debt to just $3,000.

Ralph and Pearl (Trudgeon) Jalkanen. "My father was hoist engineer for the mining company ... in Calumet, Michigan. I attended Suomi College because Professor Martii Nisonen ... gave music lessons to my family members. ... I met Ralph Jalkanen, a fellow music student [at Suomi]. The two of us often performed together. ... It was a very strict time in the Finnish Church, so when Ralph and I decided to marry, the church and college leaders ... decided that I should become a Lutheran and ought to learn Finnish. ... I would become the first non-Finnish pastor's spouse." (Pearl Jalkanen, The Way It Was 159-160)

1944

Suomi College alumna Viola (Laine) Halkola ('45) of Houghton, Michigan, recalls that during the WWII years there were very few young men on campus, with the exception of the seminarians. But the Suomi girls did not lack male companionship as Michigan Technological University hosted a training camp for the U. S. Air Force.

The October 27, 1944, issue of *Inklings* reported that the first Suomian to die in action was Paul Lepisto of Wakefield, Michigan. A Commercial Department student in 1939, Paul was the son of Mr. and Mrs. Victor Lepisto. In the same issue it was reported that future college president David Halkola, who had been reported missing in action somewhere in France, was safe. In a telegram to his parents, Rev. and Mrs. Sakari Halkola of Conneaut, Ohio, he wrote, "All my love. All well and safe. Please don't worry."

Special chapel services were held often at the college to pray for those who had died in the war or were "missing in action." Viola Halkola recalls that at one of those services, on the list of the missing was David Halkola. Although Viola hadn't met him, she says she prayed for him especially.

Viola and David met at church in January 1946, shortly after he returned from a POW camp, according to comments Viola shared in her husband's obituary in December 2009. Viola found his story fascinating. He was good-looking with curly blonde hair, too, she said, which didn't hurt. "He walked me home, and two months later, we were engaged," she said. They were married shortly after—a marriage which lasted sixty-five years.

David and Viola Halkola (left) with David's parents, Sakari and Aino Halkola, in 1947.

SEMINAARIN OPPILAAT JA OPETTAJAT V. 1944

Seminarians in 1944.

"One of the sweetest victories enjoyed by Suomi College took place in 1944. ... The game in question was with Northern Michigan University in Marquette. The only male students at Suomi were theological seminarians ... The Northern team had good-sized players, even though they were exempt from the draft. ... [but] it became apparent during the course of the game that Suomi had the better team. ... This was the only time a Suomi team faced them and walked away with a victory. The drive back to Hancock that frigid winter night was marked by elation. Even a tire change in the Upper Michigan woods didn't dampen spirits!" (The Way It Was 105)

Student life in the 1940s.

TYPING CLASS

"SOME STUDY, OTHERS DREAM"

1946

"Suomi College is now enriched by the experience of a half century. Its roots have found deeper soil. If the pioneers, an immigrant group, with few leaders to guide them, were able to establish and maintain an institution like this, much more can be expected of the generations that have become heirs to this heritage." (John Wargelin, *Golden Jubilee* 40-41)

The "New Building," as it had been called since its completion in December 1939, was finally named J.K. Nikander Hall in 1946, perhaps at the time of the college's 50th anniversary, which was celebrated June 15 to June 19 in conjunction with the annual synod convention. The college received many anniversary gifts, among them an offering of $45,000 raised by synod churches. *A Golden Jubilee Publication*, written in both English and Finnish, was published as a gift to anniversary fund donors.

For the jubilee celebration Nisonen organized and directed a Choral Festival in which choruses from across the nation participated. He also wrote and composed a dramatic presentation illustrating the different phases in the life-span of Suomi College. The music and drama programs were presented in both English and Finnish.

Speakers and special guests at the jubilee celebration included Rev. Heimer Virkkunen and Rev. Verner Aurola, both personal representatives of Archbishop Alex Lehtonen of Finland; Rev. Eino Tuori of Chicago, who had served as vice president of the Suomi Synod; and alumnus William Bilto, professor of speech at Wayne (State) University of Detroit. Other activities included a brief worship service at Lakeside Cemetery in Hancock to honor the founders of the college.

John Wargelin wrote of the constant financial worries and difficulties of the school, bemoaning the amount of time and energy spent meeting the physical needs of the school. However, he added, "this may have been a real test for the faith and the character of those who have believed in the mission of Suomi College. It has survived all difficulties with the help of God; it has provided general and vocational education on a Christian basis to thousands of youth, who otherwise might not have been able to receive it …" (*Golden Jubilee* 39)

The 50th anniversary of the college prompted much discussion about Suomi's future and her role in post-war America. "Now, at the end of its first fifty years, Suomi faces a future which contains more than the usual number of uncertainties," writes V. J. Nikander. "The need for a clear program, especially with a view to Suomi's place as an American educational institution, is urgent. For Suomi, 1946 ought to be a year of decision. … With the passing of Suomi's immigrant phase, an evaluation of the proper place of such instruction in the College's future is imperative. …"

"We propose that Suomi expand into a four-year college of liberal arts. … Suomi must set her sights high. … A four-year liberal arts college would open new avenues of training in an area where a low income average now places severe limits on the opportunities for many young people." (*Golden Jubilee* 45-50)

Nikander acknowledged the serious economic roadblocks of this plan. "Anyone burdened with the financial responsibilities of a small Christian college understands only too well the seriousness of the money problem when any form of expansion is considered." (*Golden Jubilee* 51) His dream was realized, but not until 50 years later.

A bust of Jean Sibelius was gifted to the college during the jubilee celebration.

"THIS IS THE BOOKKEEPING STUDENT. Hunched over his ledger, he is adding a mountainous column of figures. The 'peak' of his endeavors is to make a successful trial balance.' ... forty and carry the four—thirty and carry the three ... 'Debit: $10,501—Credit: $10,401 ... They didn't balance! And after five hours of slaving in numbers!! If the prospective bookkeeper is fortunate, 'Pop' Lehto will back him up with one of his snappy morale building remarks." (1948 Suomian 34-35)

In fall 1946 Nikander announced that he would resign the following July to accept a position as division head and professor in the Philosophy Department of Wagner College, Staten Island, New York.

Fall 1946 student enrollment, at 146 students, was double that of fall 1945 and the highest ever. The spring 1947 student body numbered 155, also a record. More than half of the students were veterans, most of them studying under the G.I. Bill, and the male/female gender ratio approached 2 to 1. The Commercial Department enrolled about half the students.

The Commercial Department frequently enrolled the greatest number of students and it gained an enviable reputation for producing well-trained office workers. In 1946 the course had three branches: Secretarial, Bookkeeping, and Combined. Up to 1945 Commercial graduates numbered 1003, out of a total graduate count of 1500. By 1946, a total of 4,500 students had enrolled in the college, of which 1,780 studied in the Commercial Department.

Martti Nisonen died December 5, 1946, following a short illness. He had been Suomi's music director for 25 years. Arthur J. Hill ('33), who had been hired in October of that year, became music director. Hill had completed bachelor and master of music degrees at the University of Michigan and continued his studies at Wayne University. Hill taught classes in music, music literature, music theory, voice, organ, and choir and he directed a music and choral program with a vigorous performance schedule. In 1948 Hill inaugurated an extensive annual choir tour which continued for more than a decade.

In December 1946 the Suomi College chorus sent a Christmas package to composer Jean Sibelius in Finland. The package, which included food items and Sibelius's favorite brand of cigars, had been suggested by seminarian Olaf Rankinen ('48), who had recently visited Finland. It was a time of war and strife in Finland.

The 1946-47 yearbook included a tribute to Martti Nisonen by Sibelius, who wrote in a letter to President Tamminen, "the notable and significant work done by my fellow countryman Martti Nisonen for the good of music, especially for the good of Finnish music, will continue increasingly, even now after his departure, to bear rich fruit." (December 1947 *Inklings* 3)

1948 Music Department graduate Grace Hampton playing the Nisonen Memorial Organ, a two-manual Wurlitzer series 20 organ donated to the college by the Alumni Association in 1947.

1947

The spring 1947 graduating class, at 73, was the second largest to date: 58 received Commercial Department certificates, 11 were awarded Junior College certificates, two received the first Parish Workers course certificates, and two received seminary diplomas. Six of the Junior College graduates entered the seminary that fall. Rev. Ralph J. Jalkanen, a 1943 seminary graduate and pastor of Trinity Evangelical Lutheran Church in Chicago, delivered the Commencement address on the topic, "Is It Tomorrow?"

Nikander's resignation took effect July 31, 1947. His accomplishments include the highest student enrollment in the college's history (174 students in 1946-47), the building of Nikander Hall, and two successful major fundraising campaigns, in 1942 and 1945.

On August 1, seminary graduate and board secretary Rev. Carl J. Tamminen ('27) began his duties as acting president. Tamminen had served several synod churches and was president of the Michigan Conference of the Suomi Synod. Like his predecessor, Tamminen envisioned Suomi College as a four-year institution and stressed the importance of obtaining full accreditation. In a fall 1947 poll of students, faculty, and community members the collective response to the question, "Do you think the Copper Country has a need for a four-year Liberal Arts school?" was an overwhelming yes.

For many years the month of October was designated "Suomi College Month" or "Christian Education Month" at Suomi Synod churches, and offerings that month were donated to the college. These funds, and other gifts from the synod, were relied on greatly as they represented the largest portion of dollars required for annual college operations and maintenance.

A meeting of the Suomalainen Konventti (Finnish Club) in 1947. With increasing numbers of non-Finnish students, or second and third generation Finns who had not grown up around the language, by this time the club's meetings were conducted in both Finnish and English.

Carl Tamminen in 1927 and 1948.

Business partners Les Niemi and Don Lehti tend the Nisu Nook in 1950.

1948

To foster school spirit and encourage fellowship among students in the Junior College and the Commercial Department, in fall 1948 three seminarians opened a student concession. Located in Nikander Hall and open weekday afternoons, the shop became popular and in March 1950 it was named the "Nisu Nook."

In his book *Memories*, seminary graduate Les Niemi ('54) recalls that "… We paid rent to the school for the space. … [we] offered toast, Campbell soups, candy bars, aspirin, potato chips, tee shirts, sweatshirts, and conversation. Co-eds often worked our shop for free coffee and a roll." (36)

J. K. NIKANDER HALL
Opened in December, 1939

During the summer of 1947 the college grounds were landscaped in a project led by The Martha and Mary Society. A retaining wall and cement staircase was constructed adjacent to Nikander Hall, sidewalks were laid, lawns were terraced and sodded or seeded, and a number of evergreen trees were planted.

The Suomi College Choir in 1948. The choir toured eight cities in spring 1948, departing March 27 and returning April 5: Newberry, Kaleva, and Detroit, Mich.; Warren, Fairport Harbor, Ashtabula, and Conneaut, Ohio; and DeKalb, Ill. They traveled some 2,000 miles and entertained as many as 4,000 listeners.

Suomi College students, faculty, and staff in 1948. Among this group might be Thien Karnasuta of Bangkok, Siam (Thailand), the first non-Finnish international student to enroll at Suomi. He was a student in the Commercial Department.

In 1948 flight training was offered as an elective under the G. I. Bill. Several Suomi students took advantage of the opportunity. "Contrary to common belief, flight training is not dangerous, and one doesn't have to be a reckless daredevil to be a flyer," states an article in a 1948 issue of *Inklings*.

Olaf Rankinen in 1948. "A Pastor Pilot: It sounds implausible: the Suomi Synod Air Force. But I became a pastor-pilot from 1948-1951 while serving as sole resident pastor of the Suomi Synod for all of North Dakota. The light plane I flew became a symbol of emergency Christian assistance to the people, a witness of the Evangelical Lutheran mission. ... It was apparent that a young, inexperienced, fresh Suomi College seminary graduate might be the only one who could tolerate the privations of the call. ..." (Olaf Rankinen, The Way It Was 7-8)

1949

Although WWII was over and the Korean War had not yet begun, Class of 1949 graduates were anxious about the future. "Yet, the future for this 48-49 class of graduates is not encouraging. With the country in a temporary slump, and when everybody is casting fearful eyes to the west where the march of communism is trampling over the weak and defenseless China, it seems as if we are about to graduate into times of indecision and skepticism as to the stability of our economic and military program. …." (May 1949 *Inklings* 2)

President Bernard Hillila also instructed practical theology classes.

In October 1949 Rev. Bernhard Hillila, a doctoral candidate at Union Theological Seminary, was installed as president of Suomi College, an office he held until 1952. A seminary graduate ordained in 1941, Hillila completed a bachelor's degree at Boston University and a master's at Western Reserve University. Prior to accepting the college presidency, he was pastor of a synod congregation in Brooklyn, New York, and a professor at Wagner College. His parents, Rev. and Mrs. Hugo Hillila, were also Suomi graduates.

Hillila led a reorganization of the college into three departments, all under the Junior College: Liberal Arts, Music, and Commercial. Enrollment increased sharply in 1949, then decreased during the Korean War. Another residence near the college was purchased to serve as a boys' dormitory.

From 1949 to 1953 the seminary enjoyed its largest enrollment with from 17 to 20 students each year. Some criticism was directed at the college and seminary at this time since few of the seminarians were fluent in Finnish, and detractors felt the college was not adequately teaching the language. (*Finns in North America* 114)

Hillila wrote later that he was "convinced that students received a good preparation for the Lutheran ministry at Suomi Theological Seminary in the 1930s and 1940s. Graduates may have pronounced their Greek and Hebrew with a Finnish accent, but they were well grounded in the Biblical texts." (*The Way It Was* 75)

Edward Isaac, college president from 1952 to 1954, also defended the seminary against charges that it did not attempt to teach Finnish. (*Finns in North America* 114)

In February 1949 the Suomi Lutheran Student Association began production of a weekly radio program. A 30-minute broadcast, "The Voice of the Christian Student" was aired on Saturday afternoons on WHDF of Calumet and on an Ishpeming, Michigan-area station. Programming included speakers, music, and news. The radio broadcast continued for several years. Students enthusiastically supported the program with monthly pledges and fundraisers.

"One of the professors at Suomi during those days was Dr. Uuras Saarnivaara, … a native of Finland, and an adherent to the Laestadian branch of Finnish Lutheranism, with its emphasis on personal confession and absolution," writes Bernard Hillila in *The Way It Was*.

"Those were the days of slim budgets and innovation, with the staff seeking to make do with meager facilities and equipment. In such a setting, it was not too surprising that, as students arrived for class one morning, Saarnivaara was standing on a chair at the front of the room, nailing a crosspiece to two uprights he had brought from home for a makeshift map stand. Perhaps the students' arrival distracted him, for he promptly dropped a claw hammer to the floor. Almost simultaneous with the crash on the tile floor, the professor exclaimed, 'Anteeksi, hyvä lattia!' (Forgive me, good floor.) The class too was spontaneous: 'You are forgiven!'" (76)

A lecturer, teacher, pastor, archivist, and author, Saarnivaara taught Systematic Theology, Church History, Old and New Testament, and Latin from 1939 to 1954, when he returned to Finland to become editor of Sana, a well-known Finnish religious newspaper.

1950

In the early 1950s the synod began a Church Advancement Program (CAP) in which the college participated and from which it benefitted. The small remaining debt was paid off and improvements were made to buildings and property, new books and equipment were secured for the library, and the endowment fund was increased.

HONORING . . . . . QUEEN DONNA

Donna Tuula, a Commercial Department (Accounting) major, was 1949-50 Homecoming queen. "Suomi's first Homecoming was an event that left no disappointed faces! Down the white carpet walked two solemn pages [men's basketball players in shorts and tennis shoes], followed by the Queen's attendants Doris Haryu and Margaret Lamutt. To the strains of "Pomp and Circumstance" the procession continued with Queen Donna arrayed in a white gown and the robe of royalty." (1950 *Suomian* 56)

The two-day Homecoming event continued for several decades, and was revived in the 2000s.

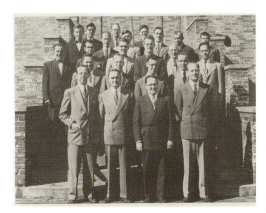

Seminary students and faculty in 1951. Seminary quarters were relocated to Old Main in fall 1950. That academic year 15 students were in the seminary, with six graduating in spring 1951.

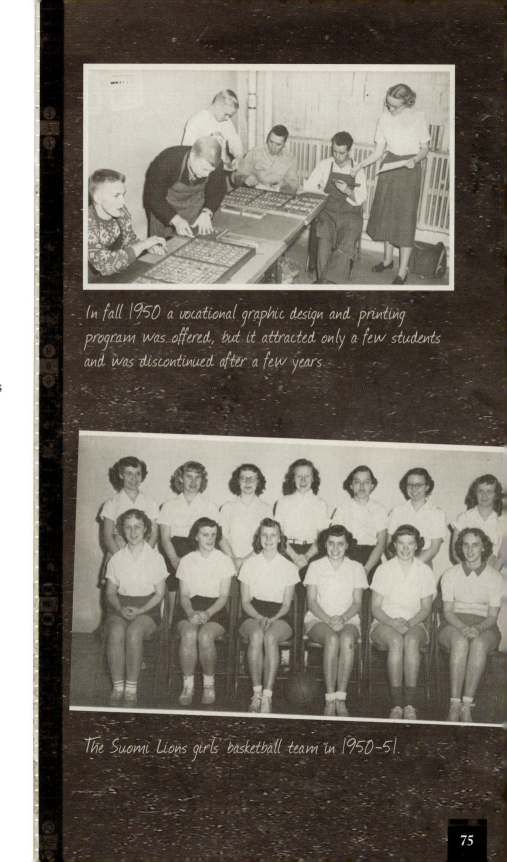

In fall 1950 a vocational graphic design and printing program was offered, but it attracted only a few students and was discontinued after a few years.

The Suomi Lions girls' basketball team in 1950-51.

CHAPTER SEVEN
1951-1960: A Controversial Merger

An annual Lenten Retreat for high school students was begun in March 1951 and continues today as L.I.F.T.! (Living in Faith Together), formerly the "Leadership School," now hosted by the Northern Great Lakes Synod of the ELCA.

"After the students had settled down to college life, several student-directed convocations were presented in which college life was depicted in skits and talent shows by the men's and women's dorms. One of the highlights was the annual all-German skit presented by the combined German I and II classes." (1951 Suomian 80)

1952

When he resigned in 1952 to complete his doctoral degree and return to Brooklyn, New York, Hillila reported to the synod that the assets of Suomi College had risen 33 percent in his three years as president, and that the buildings, equipment, and library had been improved. His additional accomplishments included the start of work of an Alumni Field, the remodeling of Old Main, and the addition of a summer internship program for seminarians.

On April 16 Pastor Edward J. Isaac, who had attended Suomi Seminary, succeeded Hillila as president. Ordained in 1921, Isaac received a B.A. degree from Tufts College and a B.D. from Mount Airy Seminary. When called to the college presidency, he was vice president of the synod and had been college registrar since 1948.

Enrollment dropped from 124 in 1951-52, to 94 in 1952-53, squeezing the budget and postponing planned repairs to Old Main. In 1952 the seminary became partially autonomous, with a dean of its own.

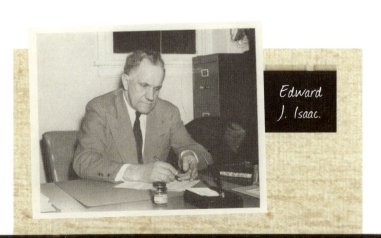

Edward J. Isaac.

LASKIAINEN

"all aboa-a-a-ard!"

Student tobogganers in 1955. In January 1952 the Student Council "has seen to it that new, eight-foot toboggans have been made available for student use. To many who will busy themselves wearing the wax from the bottom of the toboggans the faculty send its reminder that toboggan roll call will be no substitute for class roll." (January 1952 Inklings 1)

Les Niemi and Dick Rintala, 1952-53 basketball team captains.

"I averaged 24.5 points a game on the basketball court... I would be so tired from studying to 1:00 a.m., that prior to one game I made the mistake of stretching out on the bed only to discover that I had slept through the first half of a home game. ... My No. 29 jersey was retired in 1994 at the Paavo Nurmi Fieldhouse, and is lodged in the Finnish-American Archives for safekeeping." (Les Niemi, *Memories* 44-46)

"Acknowledgement of Suomi's importance in civic affairs was made by the Hancock Chamber of Commerce recently when it decided to erect a sign bearing the words 'Welcome to Hancock, Home of Suomi College.'" The sign was located on the Hancock side of the Houghton County bridge. (December 17, 1953 Inklings 1)

Holmio was the last dean of the theological seminary. He taught Finnish in the seminary from 1946 to 1958, and then for eight more years in the Junior College. He also managed the library. After retiring from teaching in 1966 to write historical works about the American Finns, he continued serving as curator of the Finnish American Archives at Suomi College. Educated at the University of Helsinki, Holmio served congregations in Finland and the U.S. and was a chaplain in the U.S. Army during WWII. He earned a Th.D. from Boston University in the field of church history.

1953

The Michigan Commission on Accreditation approved Suomi College for accreditation, which had previously been granted by University of Michigan. Waino Lehto was named dean of the Junior College and Armas Holmio was named dean of the seminary.

For decades the seminary lived a quiet life of its own, but giving a religious flavor to the entire college. Seminarians preached at college chapel services and in Copper Country churches, often accompanied by singers selected from among the college's students. The seminarians were the backbone of the Lutheran Student Association and conducted Bible study sessions. In the 1950s, after a bachelor's degree became a requirement for seminary admission, seminarians often served as part-time instructors in the Junior College.

Dr. Walter Kukkonen was dean of the seminary from 1952 to 1955.

1954

President Isaac died unexpectedly in the summer of 1954. David Halkola, a Suomi graduate and instructor of history and political science since 1948, was appointed interim president and, later that school year, acting president for a period of two years. As Halkola was not an ordained clergyman, per the college constitution he could not be named a permanent president. Halkola earned a B.A. at Wittenberg University and an M.A. at Western Reserve University.

The Suomi College Alumni Field was dedicated during Homecoming in October 1954. The field was made possible by the Alumni Association, which had been organized by John Wargelin in 1914.

In the early 1950s the Theological Seminary became a factor in the movement for a merger of various Lutheran churches in America. In 1957 Suomi Synod members voted in favor of the merger plan proposed by the Joint Commission on Lutheran Unity (JCLU), which desired to relocate the seminary and affiliate it with some larger seminary of the United Lutheran Church in America.

At the 50th annual commencement, June 6, 1954, Suomi College congratulated 34 graduates.

Class of 1904 graduates (left to right): John Wargelin, Alfred Haapanen, Minnie Perttula-Maki, and Matt Luttinen at the Suomi College 50th anniversary commencement in May 1954.

At the same time, some favored changing the constitution of Suomi College to allow a layman to serve as president, but felt that a layman should not be president of the seminary. In 1955, the seminary was granted additional autonomy and a separate budget.

Halkola found himself in the middle of a tug of war, Arnold Stadius writes in *The Finns in North America*. During the first years of Halkola's tenure, the fate of the seminary remained uncertain while the separation terms and practical details were worked out. "The situation was further complicated when the dean of the seminary applied for a longer leave of absence, another seminary instructor resigned, and a third died unexpectedly before he had delivered a single lecture." (115)

David Halkola in 1958 with Lutheran youth leaders during the annual Lenten Retreat.

Dean Lehto and students in the 1950s.

1955

At commencement exercises in 1955 Suomi College granted its first titled degrees: the associate of arts (A.A.) and the associate in commerce (A.C.).

Photo at right: Holmio officiates in this 1955 photo of a chapel service in Nikander Hall. "Chapel time at Suomi is a period of devotion, a short 'quiet-time' when the student and teacher can commune with God." (1955 Suomian 20)

Ron Arndt and Dick Rintala in the Old Main dining room in 1952-53.

1956

By 1956 some 6,200 students had attended Suomi College, about 2,000 had completed degrees, and 117 pastors had been ordained from the seminary. The school's 60th anniversary was celebrated September 7 to September 11 with an open house, alumni reunion and banquet, a performance by the Duluth Symphony Orchestra, and a massed choir performance of music by Jean Sibelius. The college constitution was modified to allow the installation of Halkola as the college's first lay president.

A 1950s Suomi College Choir performance.

Dean Lehto and other faculty and the Sampo Society in 1955. The six students are George Franti, Joan Gagnon, Arnold Perry, Joan Tamminen, Beatrice Wilminko, and Carole Wisti.

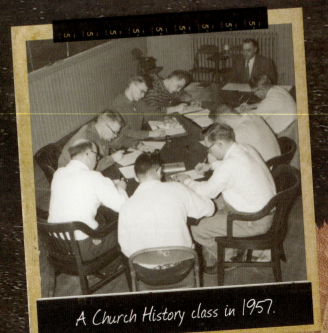

A Church History class in 1957.

1958

The question of a merger with a larger Lutheran seminary caused some controversy in the Suomi Synod, with the younger congregants in favor and the older people mostly of the opinion that the decision should be deferred until the outcome of discussions about a possible merger of the Suomi Synod with other Lutheran churches. In early 1958, the matter was voted upon by Suomi Synod members and the majority felt the seminary should remain in Hancock for the time being. But when the question came up before the June 1958 synod convention in Detroit, the younger people were in the majority and the proposal that the seminary should be merged with the Chicago Lutheran Seminary in Maywood received 167 votes to pass the measure; 149 were opposed.

In the March 1958 issue of *Inklings* students write, "We deeply regret the … decision to move the seminary from our campus. Departing she carries away with her much of our spiritual leadership. Throughout the long decades many a fresh and vital outlook in life has been given to us through her men, young men who were called to the service of God. For many of us students it is difficult to think of Suomi without the Seminary." (1)

The Suomi Seminary Class of 1954 and faculty members. In its 54-year history, 119 men were ordained from the Suomi Seminary.

The separation of Suomi College and the Theological Seminary took effect on July 1, 1958. On the same day, the seminary became affiliated with Chicago Lutheran Seminary of Maywood, Illinois. The college board selected Dr. Walter J. Kukkonen and Pastor Kaarlo Keljo to teach at Maywood as representatives of the Suomi Synod.

By 1958, English was the primary language used by both the college and the synod. "Suomi College went with the stream," Arnold Stadius writes. "American-born presidents and instructors wanted an American school for American students. They did not, however, run roughshod over the sensitive feelings of the Finnish-born, but rather tried to maintain the Finnish language as well as the Finnish background of the college. It proved impossible."

"Change of language, change of faculty, change of program. Was there in addition a change of purpose, of tradition, of spirit? The question cannot be answered with a simple 'yes' or 'no.'" (*Finns in North America* 116-117)

The 1957-58 Student Council (left to right): front row: Claire Avery, Arne Henderson, Scott Dickson, Sylvia Saari; back: Teena Mello, Douglas Niemi, James Johnson, Siegbert King, Delbert Keltto.

In fall 1958 the college welcomed 168 students, an all-time high. Pastor Martin F. Saarinen, a 1958 seminary graduate, became the college's first campus chaplain, also serving as the registrar and teaching psychology and sociology classes.

Choir Director Arthur Hill. From March 28 to April 16, 1958, the Suomi College Choir toured 18 cities, performing concerts in Arizona, California, Colorado, Minnesota, Montana, New Mexico, North Dakota, Oregon, and South Dakota.

Jean (Tamminen) Terrio, the daughter of college president Carl Tamminen, attended Suomi in 1958. She sang in the choir and took voice lessons from choir director Art Hill. "He was a good director … if you as much as looked away from him during a song, and then looked back, he would glare at you until the end of the song, and you wanted to fall through the floor," Terrio recalls.

At a concert in Crystal Falls in the early spring "the flood lights got warm and brought the flies out of hibernation," Terrio recalls. "He [Hill] would direct with his hands right in front of him, but he always mouthed the words with us. We were doing a particularly lamenting song, 'Listen to the lambs, all a-crying', when a fly flew into his mouth. A few seconds later he spit it out. Then he proceeded to glare at all of us so we would finish this most serious of songs … when we were done, we collapsed on the risers in laughter. He turned around to tell the audience what happened, and finished with, 'Oh, how I hate raw flies.'"

In those days the college was often referred to as the "shoe factory." "Everything that went in came out in pairs," Terrio says. Terrio's oldest sister met her husband at Suomi, and her brother met his wife. "My next sister went but did not meet a mate, but that didn't deter me. I went and met [my husband] Gary there."

Even first Suomi president J. K. Nikander met and married at the college. It worked for Arthur Hill, too. Martha, Hill's second wife, related this story: "Art Hill's [late] wife accompanied me when I did solo work. Not long after her death I took a job as secretary to Rev. Holmio [who] would send me down for a coffee break when Art was there—in the coffee shop. I was accepted at U of M after studying under Hill for two years, but did not go because Hill asked me to marry him." Art and Martha were married in October 1958. Martha often accompanied Art on choir trips.

Student life in the 1950s.

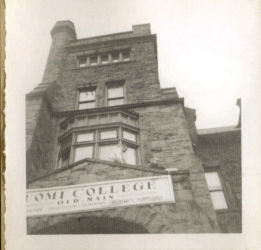
WORKING HARD?

WAITING TO SHOVE OFF.

COFFEE TIME
DOROTHY HALONEN, MARGIE LEINONEN

ELLEN TERVO, SYLVIA SAARI, TEENA MELLO, + JIM GEDROSE
BROCKWAY MOUNTAIN

SYLVIA SAARI, MARIAN WISTI, DOROTHY HALONEN, MARTHA MATTILA, ELLEN TERVO
CAUGHT IN THE ACT?

John Piirto, Dave Ochander, Warren Hill, Jim Georose.

Marian + Jim caught in the Wisti George fire escape - 1:00 A.M.

The girls + Chuck A. at Fort Wilkins

Starting for home at Christmas. Mauno, Donna, Warren Hill

Kaarlo Rintala, Clair Avery, John Bispala, Donna Wargelin + Chuck Altonen

The Suomi College choir in 1960. The choir's performance of Charles Gounod's "Gallia" in the 1959-60 season of the Worcester County (Mass.) Music Association was ranked by the association as among the top ten performances of that season. "Three college choirs from Michigan and one from Virginia visited Worcester and the area," wrote Raymond Morin. "Most memorable were the 43 voices from Suomi College of Hancock, Mich. ..." (September 1960 Inklings 2)

Rev. Dr. Raymond Wargelin.

1960

Halkola resigned the college presidency in January 1960, remaining on the faculty for a time then becoming a professor of history at Michigan Technological University. Raymond Wargelin, president of the synod, was interim college president until fall 1960 when Ralph J. Jalkanen was appointed. Jalkanen would serve as president of the college for 30 years.

Jalkanen "grew up" in the Suomi community. He is the last Suomi Seminary-trained president of the college.

Born in Hancock to Finnish immigrants, and raised in Wisconsin, Jalkanen graduated from Suomi College in 1940 and Suomi Seminary in 1943. He completed a bachelor's degree at Elmhurst College, a master's at Roosevelt University, and additional graduate study at the University of Chicago and Loyola University.

He was a clinical psychologist and a member of the American Psychological Association. Before accepting the call to become president of Suomi, Jalkanen was pastor of the Bethany Lutheran Church of Ashtabula, Ohio. He served as secretary of the synod for 17 years.

Fall 1960 semester enrollment was a record-breaking 172 students. Old Main had a new roof, made possible by The Martha and Mary Society, the college's women's auxiliary. All classes were now conducted in Nikander Hall and a new orientation plan consisted of a series of lectures by faculty to acquaint freshmen with the traditions and history of Suomi College.

" … we intend to make Suomi one of the best Junior Colleges in the Northwest," writes Jalkanen in the September 1960 issue of *Inklings*. "To do this we are launching in two different directions: first, we intend to increase our student body to optimal level. Next we shall need funds to make this a reality." (2)

A 70th Anniversary Appeal, with a goal of $100,000, was launched.

Established in 1934, by 1960 the Suomi College Martha and Mary Society raised more than $20,000 for campus improvements including the landscaping of Nikander Hall, renovation of the dormitories, and in 1960 a new roof for Old Main. The "women's auxiliary" also granted an annual scholarship to a returning sophomore female and contributed regularly to the library fund. Among the society's fundraising activities were an annual Christmas bazaar and sales of Suomi plates and stationery.

CHAPTER EIGHT

1961-1990: Three Decades of Growth

Ralph Jalkanen in 1969.

Jalkanen identified improvement of the school's financial condition as his first priority. Remarkable increased giving by new constituencies was effected through well-planned and vigorously conducted fundraising drives. By 1965 the budget was balanced and borrowed endowment funds were replaced. To bolster enrollment the offices of the registrar and admissions were strengthened, full-time recruiters were employed, thousands of recruitment brochures were printed and mailed, and the board began to sponsor academic scholarships.

However, Holmio writes, "To understand the dramatic change in the fortunes of Suomi College [in the 1960s] one must appreciate the change of purpose and philosophy. Merely to conclude that a fortuitous combination of increased enrollment and increased giving were the causes of this change would be a mistake."

Holmio identifies as key in this change an increase in board membership to represent three interest groups: educators, professionals and business people, and representatives of the history of the college and earlier supporters. Some board members were selected by supporting synods and boards, some by the college board. (*Finns in North America* 120-121)

1960s students.

1961

The fall 1961 semester marked another all-time high enrollment, 212 students, with 85 living on campus. A campus expansion program, endorsed by Michigan governor John B. Swainson and other lawmakers, was proposed. The first new building would include a dormitory, student center, dining room, and library. The cost of constructing the Student Center (later named Mannerheim Hall) was estimated at $300,000 and a fundraising drive was begun.

In the early morning of November 7 a fire broke out in the attic of Old Main. Damage was limited to the attic area and fortunately no one was injured. Immediately following, a temporary roof was installed and an emergency appeal launched. Damages were estimated at $80,000 and reconstruction began November 20. Thirty-five girls and the Old Main housemother lived in Hotel Scott while repairs took place.

The women of St. Matthew's Church of Hancock baked 1,500 pasties to raise funds to replace the dining room and bed linens destroyed in the fire. They began peeling potatoes Monday afternoon, November 14, working around the clock in what seemed "an endless day of kneading dough, rolling it out, filling the dough with meat and potatoes, and baking the pasties." Early Tuesday morning the first load of oven-ready pasties was transported to Star Bakery. The ovens at St. Matthew's Church and Old Main were also employed.

"It was a frantic rush to meet all the orders and a sacrifice on the part of the women, to whom the college means a lot. Despite the limited time to prepare for it, the pasty sale was a huge success," said Mrs. Raymond Wargelin. (November 1961 *Inklings* 1)

Firemen remain at the scene.

After the fire.

In a letter to the *Inklings* editor, a businessman staying at the Hotel Scott writes, "I wish to congratulate you upon your group of coeds … the fortitude of your students … was amazing … they called upon their Christian strength and avoided panic … I also understand that your boys proved to be Men … aiding the girls and seeing to it that the records and … college equipment … was removed from the danger of flames. … I'm proud that I was able to view this Christian act … in person. … you and your staff can be congratulated for helping to mold such morale." (November 1961 *Inklings* 2)

Left: 1959-60 Dramatics Club.
Below: Choir members in 1960-61.

College secretaries Sylvia Koski and Joan Chamberlain in the 1960s. In 2012 Koski said she believes that the Old Main fire may have been set by a student who was seeking attention, although the actual cause of the fire is unknown. Koski, hired by President V. K. Nikander, retired in 1992 following 45 years as a secretary and bookkeeper for the college.

1961-62 residents of the Burritt House.

Row 1: Lynn Stauffacher, Jack Weatherwax, Dave Aho, Dale Quasius, Bob Van Abel, Walter Kinnunen.
Row 2: Francis Ahlman, Mal Tygesson, Dennis Matchinski, John Dobbs.
Row 3: Bruce Maki, Richard Gilstorf, Jack Kelly, Richard Palmer, Dave Johnson.

1960-61 students.

Alma Van Slyke, pictured in 1923 and 1965, was dean of women from 1922 to 1925, returning to Suomi in 1956 to teach English, literature, and library science. Laurel (Manzetti) Gauthier, who attended Suomi from 1960 to 1962, recalls that Van Slyke was very knowledgeable about English language and literature. "You'd see her climb to the top of the stairs and think she was about to take her last breath, and then she would begin to recite poetry—maybe 100 lines—from memory! She had more poetry memorized than I read in my whole life."

Waino "Pop" Lehto with students in the 1950s.

1962

Old Main was reopened February 4, 1962, with an open house, and a ceremony presented in both English and Finnish. In fall 1962 enrollment climbed to 221 students, another record.

After 39 years, at the conclusion of the 1961-62 academic year, Waino "Pop" Lehto celebrated his 65th birthday and retired.

As head of the Commercial Department, the first dean of the Junior College, and instructor, "he has brought much distinction to the school through his long, faithful, and most competent efforts. He has made the fine quality of his teaching and the promotion of Suomi his life work; [he] has had an influence on all those with whom he has had contact."

"'Give me your ears.' These words will be remembered by Suomi's commercial students long after they have graduated, and these same words will bring them many happy memories of the person to whom they belong, Mr. Waino Lehto." (1962 *Suomian* 7)

Carl Waisanen was appointed Commercial Department dean in fall 1962, serving as instructor and dean until his retirement in April 1987.

"Pop" Lehto and Elizabeth (Tuori) Lehto both taught at Suomi for more than 40 years. Waino was liked and respected by his students and he was known on campus as "Pop" Lehto. Although some sources say "Pops," according to his son, Paul Lehto, it was "Pop." (Photo courtesy of the Lehto family.)

The Homecoming 1974 dance.

"With the coming of the 1962-63 school year there have been many changes in school policy. A predominant one is that of dancing at Suomi. This never heard of thing has finally come …" says a letter from the Student Council in the November 1962 issue of *Inklings*. (2)

The evening of November 3, 1962, "the students [at] Suomi College … took a step forward, and left an imprint that will be embedded in the school's history forever. They organized and attended the first dance ever to be held at Suomi." The semi-formal affair was held in the in Nikander Hall gymnasium, which was decorated with "grape-like clusters of balloons and long streams of crepe paper." Small tables placed along the sidelines offered "sequestered abodes in which couples could relax" and enjoy punch and snacks. Music by the Starlighter Combo varied from "slow waltzes to explosive twists." (8)

1963

In January, Suomi College and the Finnish Evangelical Lutheran Church of America (Suomi Synod) affiliated with the newly constituted Lutheran Church in America (LCA), a merger of the Suomi Synod, The American Evangelical Lutheran Church, The Augustana Evangelical Lutheran Church, and The United Lutheran Church in America.

Some LCA officials felt that the school's remote location would make it difficult, if not impossible to sustain, pressuring the college board to relocate the college or close its doors. "Dr. Raymond Wargelin, last president of the Synod and former president of the college, eloquently and effectively pleaded the case for continuing Suomi College in Hancock. … He spoke objectively about the institution's future and pointed out that Suomi was the only significant visible symbol of the life and work of the Finnish people in this country." (*Faith of the Finns* 314)

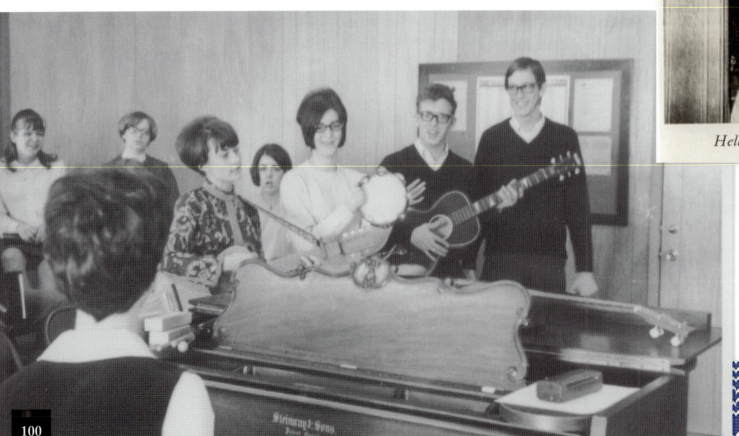

Hello!? Sorry! Wrong number.

Above: 1961-62 students crowd into a phone booth.

Left: Student musicians in the 1960s.

The Suomi Choir in Finland in 1963.

At the invitation of the Lutheran World Federation, the Suomi College Choir, augmented with choir alumni and directed by Art Hill, performed at the federation's Fourth Assembly in Helsinki. The July 30 to August 10, 1963, tour also included performances at churches in Finland, Germany, Sweden, and Denmark, and visits with Archbishop Ilmari Salomies in Turku and with Finland president Urho Kekkonen at his summer home in Kultaranta. Jalkanen traveled with the choir.

Now as part of the LCA, the college could draw on financial support from a wider constituency. Initially assigned to both the Wisconsin-Upper Michigan Synod and the Michigan Synod, in 1965 college affiliation was assigned to the LCA Board of College Education.

"This past year … has been a year of historic significance for Suomi," Jalkanen writes to graduates in the 1963 *Suomian*. "You have witnessed our merger into the Lutheran Church in America, with a constituency of 3,200,000 members. During your residence here, final plans for the proposed Dormitory-Student Center have been made. The College is entering a period of dynamic growth." (6)

A 1960s aerial view of campus. Nikander Hall is the left-most building, the Student Center is adjacent, and Wargelin Hall, under construction, is at the far right. Note that the Paavo Nurmi Center and Finlandia Hall haven't yet been built.

1964

At a special meeting in November 1964 the college board voted to accept a $450,000 loan from the federal Housing and Home Finance Agency to construct the Student Center. Groundbreaking took place May 30.

The first annual Alumni Smorgasbord was hosted in March 1964. The spring banquets continued for more than 20 years, serving greater than 1,000 diners each year and raising thousands of dollars for student scholarships. Pictured is the crowd at the 1985 dinner in the Paavo Nurmi Center gymnasium.

A Commercial Department class in the 1960s.

1965

The Suomi College Student Center (later named Mannerheim Hall) was dedicated May 29 in conjunction with commencement and an Alumni Weekend. The final cost of the building and fixtures was about $575,000. Two wings of double-occupancy dormitory rooms—to house up to 106 students in each wing—were separated by a dining hall (with fireplace), lounges, conference rooms, and a student center.

Of special significance, as reported in the March 1965 issue of *Inklings*, was the snack bar and Lions' Den student center. "The former will be open all day for student use and the latter is a special room; it will contain a ping pong table plus tables and chairs … not ordinary tables and chairs, however, but the kind you may probably initial if you wish."

The sixty-year-old Lutheran Book Concern building was acquired in 1965 and used for art, music, commercial, and other classes into the 1990s; it was demolished in the early 2000s.

Above: 1964-65 students on a fall color tour.

Left: Students celebrate the opening of the Student Center in 1965.

Winning Year For Lions

LEFT TO RIGHT, KNEELING: Ray Malila, Fred Ranta, Marty Logan, Charles Smith, Ronald Leipsto, Robert Doern—Manager.
STANDING: Thomas Renier—Coach, Robert Ziemnick, Dennis Miilee, George Hausske, Mark Schroeder, John Veres, Dennis Poyhonen, Jim Ahola—Manager.

In January 1965, for the first time in college history, the men's basketball team received regional recognition, ranking second in wins and offensive points per game among 22 colleges in Upper Michigan, Minnesota, Montana, and North and South Dakota. It was the first of many accolades for the team and Coach Tom Renier.

Far left: 1964-65 students at the state capitol in Lansing, Michigan.

Left: Two students study in 1965.

Wargelin Hall construction.

Wargelin Hall was completed in 1967.

1966

The cornerstone for Wargelin Hall, a new library and science building, was placed September 28, 1966. The building, completed in 1967, is named for John Wargelin, the second president of Suomi College.

Pictured are (left to right): Russell Hoyer, Pr. John Juntilla, Onni Malila, and Melvin Hagelberg.

Left: The Wargelin Hall library prior to its renovation and expansion in 1997.

Below: The Wargelin Hall lecture hall, still the largest lecture hall on campus, seats 144.

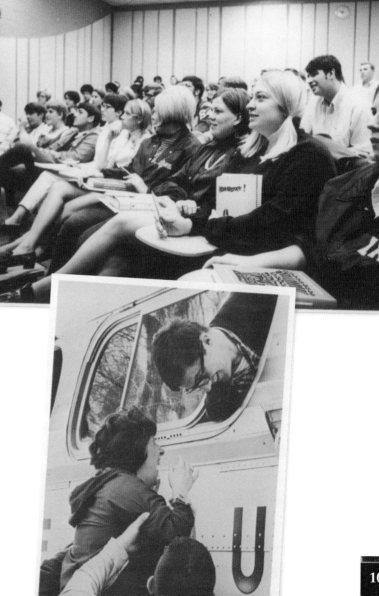

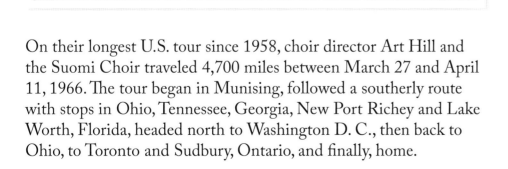

On their longest U.S. tour since 1958, choir director Art Hill and the Suomi Choir traveled 4,700 miles between March 27 and April 11, 1966. The tour began in Munising, followed a southerly route with stops in Ohio, Tennessee, Georgia, New Port Richey and Lake Worth, Florida, headed north to Washington D. C., then back to Ohio, to Toronto and Sudbury, Ontario, and finally, home.

The Paavo Nurmi Center groundbreaking ceremony was February 25, 1966. Pictured are (left to right): President Jalkanen, board members Russell Hoyer and Onni Malila, Bert Nuranen, and Fr. Bourgeois. Plans for the multi-level structure included a full-size gymnasium and an Olympic-size swimming pool.

The Robinson House placed first in the 1968-69 Skit Night with "A Day in the Administration Office."

1969

At a March 26, 1969, meeting of the North Central Association in Chicago, Suomi College was approved for full accreditation. Jalkanen says in the May 1969 *Inklings*, "Elevation to membership in the North Central Association means that Suomi College has come of age, as judged by its educational peers, and has been recognized as meeting all the high qualifications of [the] accrediting association. This achievement marks a significant milestone in the history of the College, and recognition of its quality programs." (1)

Dean Waisanen, speaking for the faculty, said, "To achieve accreditation in the midst of the careful scrutiny which modern techniques afford, is a significant step in the life of any institution. The hurdles placed before the newcomer in education today are stringent indeed, and we are pleased to have performed so well against such great odds." (1)

Student David Snyder ('69) said, "All of us have been up-tight concerning regional approval, because the students here have always felt that Suomi is doing a superb job, and this is like putting 'sterling' on the silver. Suomi sure has class." (1)

Articles in the 1969 and early 1970s issues of *Inklings* explored current topics including the Vietnam War draft and women's equality. The first nationwide "Moratorium to End the War in Vietnam" of October 15 was acknowledged on campus with an open forum at which students had the opportunity to freely express their views about the southeast Asia conflict, which ranged from advocacy for complete withdrawal of U.S. troops to support for continued U.S. involvement. The start of an ROTC collaboration with Michigan Technological University also generated discussion.

Arthur Hill, Suomi College choir director since 1946, retired in spring 1968.

MR. ARTHUR J. HILL . . . Director of Suomi College's music department.

Right: 1969 graduate David Snyder.

Below: Some of the girls who resided in the Hillside House dormitory in 1969-70.

The Young Republicans and the Young Democrats clubs in 1968-69.

Left: In a presentation to the Konventti Club in 1969 Armas Holmio (pictured) reported that the college archives contained over 15,000 items, including books, newspapers, meeting minutes, and collections of poems, plays, and songs.

Dedicated November 23, 1969, the $1.25 million Paavo Nurmi Athletic Center is named for the "Flying Finn," the 1920s Finnish distance runner and Olympic gold and silver medalist. A major portion of the building sits on solid bedrock.

Its 94 x 50 hardwood gymnasium floor was "one of the finest in Michigan," and the gymnasium could seat as many as 2,000 people, at the time the largest capacity space north of the Portage Lift Bridge. (October 1969 *Inklings*)

The Olympic-size indoor heated swimming pool had a maximum depth of nine-feet, and a four-lane bowling alley was donated by the Brunswick Corp. The bowling alley was later converted to a fitness center and the pool is no longer in use. The building also houses classrooms and offices.

1970

In the 1960s, 1970s, and 1980s students resided in Old Main, four floors of the Student Center, and in Brown House, Burritt House, Elm House, Faller House, Finn House, Givens House, Hedge House, Hillside House, Holland House, the Hotel Scott, Michelson House, Mid-Town House, Pacific House, Quincy House, Robinson House, Ryan House, Suomi House, Summit House, Tomei House, Top O'Ryan House, Vieras House, and White House.

A "Finn Fair," August 6 to August 8, 1971, began Suomi's 75th Jubilee year. Miss Finland, Pirjo Laitila, was a special guest.

The 1969-70 Student Council.

1969-70 Hillside House residents.

Student groups and organizations during these years, some of them established decades before, included the Black Student Coalition, Bowling Club, Chapel Club, Cheerleaders, Commuter Club, Creative Writing Club, Delta Psi Omega (drama fraternity), dorm councils, Drama/Dramatics Club, German Club, *Inklings* staff, intramural sports, library staff, Lutheran Student Association, pool staff, Radio Club, which broadcast popular music in the late evening, resident assistants, ROTC, Science Club, Snack Bar staff, Student Council, Suomi Choir, Suomi Singers, Vets' Club, Young Democrats, Young Republicans, and yearbook staff.

Annual student events and traditions included freshmen initiation, convocations, Homecoming, Laskiainen Day, skit night, once- or twice-yearly plays, an annual musical, choir tours and local and regional choir performances, hay rides, fall color tours, spring outings, and Halloween parties.

Men's basketball in 1970-71.

Instructor Olaf Rankinen and students.

Resident assistants in 1972-73; dean of students David Strang is standing, second from the left.

1970s marketing image.

1971

A Law Enforcement Education Program (LEEP), later to become the college's criminal justice program, began in fall 1971. Graduates of the two-year course were awarded an associate of arts degree. In 1972, 44 men and seven women were enrolled in the program.

"A lot of student unrest has caused the administration to think this is going to be a 'very trying year,'" write students in a December 1971 *Inklings* article. "But just for the record, one of the beautiful things that has not been published is the Bible Study Class that takes place Wednesdays at 3:00 o'clock." (2)

Arnold Lack, assistant to the president from 1971 to 1978, recalls that Jalkanen made people feel that nobody was more important than the person he was speaking to at the time, but when "he [Ralph] was ready, he was ready RIGHT NOW." Lack describes Jalkanen as influential in his professional development and success. "He took good care of me and my wife Carolyn. It was a pleasure to work for and with him. We stayed in touch and I preached at his funeral."

1972

Several hundred Micronesians attended and graduated from Suomi in the 1970s, most of them "traditional" students in their 20s. David Strang, dean of students from 1972 to 1977, and his wife Donna, worked closely with them. Strang recalls that this new population of Suomi students necessitated cultural adjustments both for the Pacific Islanders and for the college. Special orientation programs were conducted and a Micronesian student council, based on the students' traditional tribal culture, was developed and became a national model. Each fall the Micronesian students presented in traditional costumes a program of dance and music and prepared a typical Pacific Island meal.

Ninety academic degrees and certificates were awarded at the 75th Jubilee commencement in June 1972.

2nd FLOOR OLD MAIN: Sandy, Kathy, Sue, Mary, Tracy, Lael, Kathy, Maria, Cindy, Anita, Helen, Marsha, Matie, Debra

Above: Residents of second floor Old Main in 1972-73.
Left: A 1970s science class with instructor Reino Ranta.

1973

Nikander Hall remodeling was completed in September 1973, which improved fire safety, converted the gymnasium into a multi-purpose area named the White Pine Room, and provided upper floor classrooms.

A 1973-74 student.

A student with art and design instructor and dean Jon Brookhouse in the 1970s.

1974-75 commuter students.

1974

Starting in 1974 and continuing for a number of years, off-campus instruction was offered at the Keweenaw Bay Indian Tribal Center, Baraga, Michigan. A shorter-lived program at the Keweenaw Air Force base in Calumet, Michigan, also began in 1974.

Above: 1974-75 men's basketball team and cheerleaders.
Right: Cheerleaders in 1975-76.

1976

On April 25, 1976, graduates of the largest class to date in college history were awarded 118 associate of arts degrees and seven accounting and secretarial certificates.

FinnFest '76 was hosted by Suomi College from July 29 to August 1, 1976. Distinguished guests included Finland president Urho K. Kekkonen.

Above: A group performs traditional folk dances at FinnFest '76.

Jalkanen greets Finland president Urho Kekkonen (right) in July 1976.

Left: Finland president Urho Kekkonen received the Suomi Copper Lion Award during FinnFest '76.

In spring 1976 Suomi students and community members presented the Finnish musical "Tukkilaiset" (The Lumberjacks' Life) to more than 1,100 people at the Calumet Theatre. It was the first English-language adaptation of the play, which depicts river lumberjacks, their girlfriends, and the villagers of Finland's Oulu River district in the 1890s. The play was translated into English by Suomi Finnish teacher Ritva Heikkilä. It was restaged during FinnFest '76.

Finnish instructor Ritva Heikkilä conducts a class on the lawn between Wargelin and Nikander Halls. Pictured are (left to right): Diane Nelson, Kathy Gervais Lahti, Linda Vickstrom, Susie Leppanen, Billie Leppanen, Mike Liimatta, and Heikkilä.

Waino Lehto, retired Commercial Department dean and instructor, died February 12, 1977, at age 84. Hundreds of Suomi alumni attended his funeral service in Hancock, where Jalkanen delivered the eulogy and the Suomi Choir and congregation sang Lehto's hymn, "Hail to Thee, Suomi."

Ralph and Pearl Jalkanen with President Gerald and Betty Ford in 1976 in Washington D.C.

The 1976-77 Student Council (left to right): back row: John Hyry, Carroll Bartlette, Terry Taavola, Christian Wolf, Cynthia Cross, Gordon Rice, Jim Kurtti, Valerie Hulkonen; in front: Joy Marshall on John Seiler's feet, Becky Mattila looking between Joy and John, Dean David Strang (dean of students) holding Deb Harrison upside down, Angie Harris, senate president Jim Frieson, and Gus Kailing.

Above: An intercollegiate women's basketball team was organized in the 1977-78 academic year. Pictured is the 1978-79 team with longtime coach Carol Dolata (back row, far left).

Right: Kitchen staff in 1972 (left to right): Maria Ranta, Anna Kangas, Martha Taurianen, and Alice Holombo.

1970s students.

1978

The men's basketball team, coached by Tom Renier, won the Upper Peninsula District Tournament in March 1978, defeating Gogebic Community College 115-73. The contest was the climax of a 17-2 win-loss record for the Lions that season. Suomi was ranked first in win-loss percentage in Region 13, and fourth in the regional National Junior College Athletic Association.

Community classes and camps drew a record of about 1,200 people of all ages to campus in summer 1978. Activities in addition to summer semester classes included an exhibit of historical photographs curated by the Detroit Institute of Arts, youth basketball and golf camps, martial arts and karate classes, art classes, swimming and water safety courses, the annual youth Christian Leadership School, and a Family College Day.

In fall 1978 college enrollment increased 30% to an all-time high of 504 students, which was contrary to national enrollment curves for private colleges at that time. Every dormitory and lodging space was filled to capacity. "The Old Main lot and nearby streets were jammed with cars, trailers, people, and traffic … as parents and friends helped students move into assigned residences." (September 1978 *Bridge* 1)

Exterior and interior restorations of Old Main were completed in September 1978. The $152,000 project was accomplished through a $15,000 grant from the Michigan History Division, a $70,200 federal matching grant from the Heritage Conservation and Recreation Service, and gifts from friends of the college.

Mae Shoup, a college housemother from 1968 to 1982. "Mae Shoup has been at Suomi for many years. She kept peace at Old Main by guarding the girls against the prowls of the men at night (kept them off the floors after hours). She is a wonderful person." (1978 *Suomian* 55)

Left: Students at McLain State Park in the 1970s.

Students perform in the play "Two by Two" in 1978-79.

1979

In spring 1979 the college purchased the "Lieblein Mansion" and grounds from Suomi alumnus Edward M. Lieblein, Jr., and his wife, Mary. The three-story Queen Anne-style house was built in 1895 by the senior Edward Lieblein, a wholesale grocer. The family lived in the home for 80 years. The Hoover Center is named for college trustee Vaino Hoover and his wife, Judith, whose generosity made the purchase possible. College administrative offices were relocated to the Hoover Center and the first floor of Old Main was remodeled into nine women's dorm rooms, with new bathrooms, laundry room, reception area, conference room, and an apartment for the housemother. Existing women's dorm rooms on the third floor were refurnished.

The college's 75th jubilee commencement was celebrated April 28, 1979. James R. Crumley, Jr., president of the Lutheran Church in America, congratulated 117 graduates. In July 1979 the North Central Association renewed the college's accreditation for 10 years, the maximum period granted.

Suomi opened its 85th academic year in fall 1979 with a record 570 students.

Girls' Basketball Schedule 1978-79

Today, the Hoover Center is home to the offices of the President, Institutional Advancement, Alumni Relations, and Communications and Marketing. It is just east of Old Main at the corner of U.S. 41 and Ryan Street.

The Lieblein mansion within the circle.

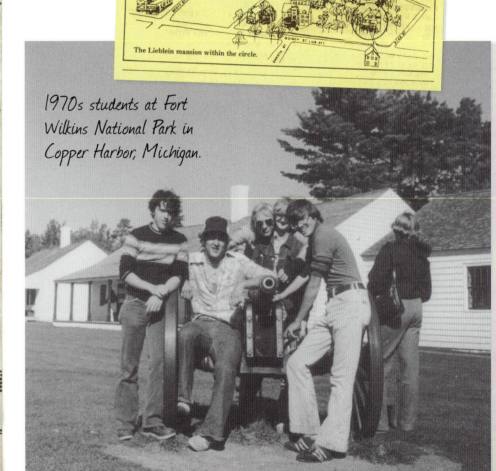

1970s students at Fort Wilkins National Park in Copper Harbor, Michigan.

1980

The college acquired the church, rectory, and property of the former St. Joseph and St. Patrick Roman Catholic Church in 1980. Just east of the Hoover Center on 1.2 acres, the former church, built in 1885, was partially remodeled in 1983 to house nursing program classrooms and labs. The building was again renovated in 1990 and is now the Finnish American Heritage Center. The rectory, which served as a student dormitory for a short time, now houses North Wind Books, the college bookstore.

Vaino Hoover (1905-1983) was a longtime member of the Suomi College board of trustees. "His concern for Finnish American culture was unbounded …" (September 1983 *Bridge*) Hoover was vice president of the American Scandinavian Foundation, and the second president of the Finlandia Foundation.

In 1980 college trustee Onni Malila ('29), on behalf of his family and descendants, pledged one million pennies ($10,000) to the "Call to Commitment Campaign." The first installment of the gift was delivered by trustee Ken Seaton in an "ore tram" at that year's alumni banquet.

The former St. Joseph and St. Patrick Roman Catholic Church.

1981

Finland president Urho Kekkonen served as official "Patron" for the school during its 85th anniversary year.

"The year 1981 marks the celebration of 85 years of history during which Suomi College has sought to provide quality education and opportunity to generations of young people," writes Jalkanen in the March 1981 *Bridge* (which was published in both English and Finnish). "The observance reminds us of the HERITAGE of 'sisu,' of sacrifice, of selfless service, and of generosity in the midst of poverty that have made it possible for Suomi to endure and thrive under difficult conditions.

"At the same time we are celebrating HOPE for the future that Suomi's students continue to carry with them wherever they go in their lives and careers." (1)

There were 125 graduates that spring.

The TRiO Upward Bound program at Suomi began in 1981. Then, as now, the U.S. Department of Education-funded program seeks to motivate high school students from modest income backgrounds to pursue post-secondary education. The program serves students in Baraga, Houghton, and Keweenaw counties. A second TRiO program, Education Talent Search, was started at Suomi in 1977, and a third, Student Support Services, in 1985.

The 85th anniversary theme was "A Lasting Heritage and Bright Hope." Donors responding to a special 85th anniversary appeal received a copper-plated medallion which depicted Old Main on one side and the Lion of Finland on the reverse. The college hosted more than 50 "Heritage & Hope" programs nationwide as part of a four-year, $2.5 million "Call to Commitment" campaign.

In August 1981, 47 people from seven states traveled to Hancock for the first-ever Elderhostel program at Suomi College. The elders attended courses including Copper Country nature, Raku pottery, folk history, and immigrant studies. This photo is of an Elderhostel group in June 1984. "Elderhostel students are much better than traditional students," says Suomi English instructor Lauri Anderson in the September 1989 *Bridge*. "They ask good questions, penetrating questions. You have to know your stuff when you teach Elderhostel." (12)

Ever mindful of the artful, head chef Don Peryam poses with an array of vegetables that was undone by students in 30 seconds once cooking class was begun.

Right: Now retired, longtime food service director Don Peryam ('69) started his position at Suomi in 1981. "You eat with your eyes long before you even taste the food," he says in the September 1987 Bridge. "So even if we serve chili, the table will be gorgeous." Peryam also instructed food preparation and sanitation classes for Suomi's hotel and restaurant management program.

1982

A nurses' aide health training program was begun in February 1982, following discontinuance of the nursing program at Michigan Technological University. Two-year degrees in medical assisting and travel services were begun in fall 1982.

In August 1982 more than 500 people visited campus for "Mini-Fest '82," a three-day festival of Finnish music and culture. Activities included a performance by the Hoijakat folk dancers and a ten-foot "kokko" fire built by Arvo Pyörälä, "Hot Line Charlie."

Bernhard Hillila, college president from 1949 to 1952, delivered the 85th anniversary commencement address and was awarded the Suomi Copper Lion Award.

The college enrolled a record 600 students in fall 1982. Reflecting popular culture of the times, a chapel service that fall was attended by E.T.s (extra-terrestrials). The sermon topic, "The Gospel According to E.T.," explored parallels between fictional characters and modern society. The student E.T.s are Scott Owen and Beth Raatz."

1983

The college designated 1983 "The Year of the Archives" and a national effort was begun to gather materials and funds to preserve the Suomi College Finnish American Historical Archives. At the same time, a United Fund for Finnish American Archives (UFFAA) was established to build and preserve the archive collections of Suomi's archive and the Immigration History Research Center at the University of Minnesota. The initial aim of the UFFAA was to microfilm copies of the Finnish language newspapers in both archives.

The college's Finnish Council in America was founded July 29, 1983. The first major undertaking of the new council was leading the organization of "Gala Kaleva," FinnFest USA '85.

"Are you proud of your Finnishness? Are you willing to devote a part of your energy on behalf of your heritage? Or is your Finnish-ness your best kept secret?" asks an article in a special section of the December 1983 *Bridge*. "The Finnish Council intends to 'network' concerning things Finnish. How do we plan for the well-being of the Finnish ethnic presence in America? How can we live out our heritage? The Finnish Council wishes to have us say, 'It's O.K. to be Finnish.'"

The Michigan State Board of Nursing granted preliminary approval to Suomi's two-year registered nursing program in summer 1983. The program began that fall with the help of a $160,000 grant from the U.S. Department of Education. In 1988, following a required a five-year probationary period, the nursing program received full Michigan State Board approval.

Several hundred people attended a Finn Faith Forum at the college July 29 to July 31, 1983. The three-day event featured six theologians, three of them graduates of the Helsinki School of Theology. A book generated from the forum, "… And I'll Take the Low Road," co-edited by Jalkanen and Walter Kukkonen, was published in 1985. Raymond Wargelin, pictured with Onni Malila, was presented with the Suomi College Founder's Award at the event. Raymond Wargelin was a professor of practical theology at Suomi Seminary from 1943 to 1946, a member of the college board from 1948 to 1952, and college president in 1959 and 1960. He was president of the Suomi Synod from 1955 to 1962.

Groundbreaking for Finlandia Hall took place April 24, 1983, and construction began the following June. The building, just west of the Paavo Nurmi Center, was designed by TMP Associates of Bloomfield Hills, Michigan, which was awarded two trade association awards for its design of the building.

Suomi College faculty in 1983.

Above: The Martha and Mary Society celebrated its 50th anniversary of service to Suomi College November 17, 1984.

1984

At 156 graduates, the 80th graduating class was the largest to date. The Class of 1984 accepted their diplomas April 29.

Fall 1984 enrollment rose to another all-time high, at 679 students. It was the first time enrollment surpassed 600. Seventy-four students enrolled in the new nursing program (29 of them working parents). About 70% of all students were enrolled in the business department, which included programs in data processing, law enforcement, travel and tourism, and medical assisting. Thirty-seven percent came from the Upper Peninsula, 35% from lower Michigan, and international students represented the countries of Canada, Japan, Kuwait, Nigeria, Malaysia, and Micronesia.

In fall 1984 the Finlandia Hall dormitory was completed. At the September 29 dedication Jalkanen said that the Finnish traits of perseverance, endurance, and a stick-to-it attitude made the construction possible "It took those traits to get the $3.5 million dormitory built," Jalkanen is paraphrased as saying in the December 1984 *Bridge*. "Suomi applied for a federal construction loan 12 times before it was finally approved," concluding philosophically that "behind every success there are many failures." (1)

General contractor for the Finlandia Hall project, Herman Gundlach, said at the dedication, "Bricks and mortar, budgets and bucks, only scratch the surface of what Suomi is all about. … I also salute Suomi as a builder—a builder of our citizens, a builder of our students, and a builder of our area economy." (December 1984 *Bridge* 1)

A 1980s aerial view of Hancock and the college campus.

1985

Loret Miller Ruppe (1936-1996), director of the Peace Corps from 1981 to 1989, addressed the Class of 1985 at commencement April 28. She urged the record graduating class of 176 students to work for world peace, saying, "Peace—that beautiful five-letter word which we all treasure and pray for—is up for grabs in the 80s." (June 1985 *Bridge* 1) Today, the Philip and Loret Ruppe Community Service Scholarship is awarded annually to one or more students to commemorate the service of former Congressman Phil Ruppe, a Houghton, Michigan, native, and his wife, Loret Ruppe.

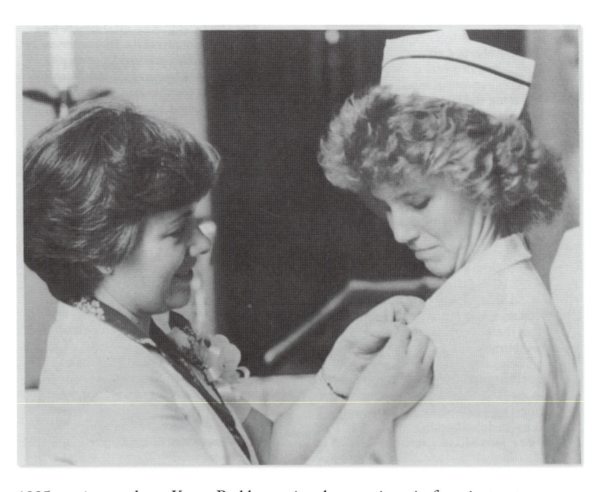

Loret Miller Ruppe was awarded the Suomi College Copper Lion Award in 1985.

1985 nursing graduate Karen Porkka receives her nursing pin from instructor Barbara Whitman April 27. The Class of 1985 included the first 29 graduates of the college's nursing program. From 1985 to 2005, 463 students graduated from the A.D.N. program.

In March 1985 Church of Finland archbishop Rev. John Vickström visited Suomi as part of a U.S. tour. Vickström was the third Church of Finland archbishop to visit the college.

Men's basketball coach Tom Renier celebrated his 300th career victory in a 71-69 win over Northland College in the final game of the 1984-85 season.

Brenda Sue Blevins and Brad Nielsen were 1984-85 Homecoming queen and king.

Team Finland defeated the Suomi College Lions, 99-66, at an exhibition game in fall 1985, which nearly 1,000 people attended.

FinnFest USA '85 was hosted by Suomi College July 25 to 28. Drawing more than 5,000 visitors, the festival celebrated the 150th anniversary of *The Kalevala*, Finland's national epic. Three internationally-known *Kalevala* scholars participated and Finland's minister of education designated Suomi College as the official site for celebration of the 150th anniversary of the publication of the *Kalevala*. July 21 to July 27, 1985, was declared Finnish Heritage Week by Michigan governor James Blanchard.

A play about Upper Peninsula Finnish immigrants, written for FinnFest '85 by Kentucky playwright William Tyler Thomas, was performed July 26. The play, "Kuparisaari Kultamaa/Copper Island, Land of Gold," is based on oral histories from the Suomi College archive collections. Suomi College music and drama instructor Melvin Kangas composed music for the production. The play was also presented at FinnFest '87 in Detroit. In 2004 the Michigan Humanities Council selected the play as one of 30 "Outstanding Humanities Projects" funded by the council in its 30-year history.

In a fourth consecutive year of record enrollment, 697 students were welcomed in fall 1985. Other fall 1985 milestones were the largest number of full-time students (645), the largest number of resident students (466), and the largest sophomore class (232).

Dick Enberg and Lasse Viren

Sportscaster Dick Enberg, who is of Finnish descent, was master of ceremonies for FinnFest '85 closing ceremonies. Enberg served a three-year term on the Suomi College board of trustees, from 1984 to 1986.

Finnish line of Canal Run

Finnish organizations at opening

Finnish folk dancers

Opening ceremony

"The trumpets bugled the fanfare, and the murmuring people quieted, expectant and excited. The drums rolled in cadence. The march began. The audience stood. FinnFest USA, 1985 was underway.

"The pomp and circumstance, music, speech and dance lasted two hours as 3,500 people celebrated the charms of being Finnish and sang the praises of the 'land most dearly loved, cherished Suomiland.' The Governor of Michigan praised Finns. Finns praised fellow Finns. Everybody was at least Finn for a day."

(September 1985 Bridge 5)

An expanded intramural sports program, begun in 1986, included cross-country skiing, bowling, and basketball.

1986

Spring 1986 commencement celebrated another banner year of graduates, with 190.

In June 1986 the college board voted to discontinue men's and women's intercollegiate basketball in favor of expanding existing intramural athletics. "The general philosophy behind the move is that we want … more opportunity for more involvement for more students," says academic dean Don Myrvik in the June 1986 *Bridge*, explaining that the intramural program would be expanded to seven days a week and include three dozen sport and recreational programs. (2)

Tom Renier was head coach of the Suomi College men's basketball team from 1963 to 1986, achieving more than 300 victories and a combined record of 308 wins and 159 losses. Achievements under Renier's 23-year tenure include 12 National Junior College Athletic Association (NJCAA) district and/or sub-regional titles, including four seasons ranked first in Region XIII (1970-71, 1977-78, 1978-79, and 1979-80). Most notably, Renier's 1979-80 team finished with a 19-1 record and earned a runner-up finish in the NJCAA Regional XIII Championship.

Suomi's 90th anniversary was celebrated in fall 1986; 615 were enrolled and a two-year program in hotel and restaurant management began. In October Finland's ambassador to the United States, Paavo Tantanen, visited campus.

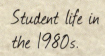

Student life in the 1980s.

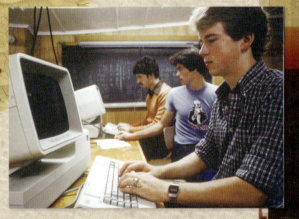

1987

A merger of the American Lutheran Church, the Association of Evangelical Lutheran Churches, and the Lutheran Church in America—three of the four largest divisions of the Lutheran church in the U.S.—was finalized in spring 1987 to take effect in January 1988. The united groups became the Evangelical Lutheran Church in America.

In summer 1987, with a $350,000 low-interest loan from the U.S. Department of Housing and Urban Development, two major remodeling projects were completed. At Old Main, the roof and windows were replaced. At the Student Center (Mannerheim Hall), built in 1963, the roof and outside walls were insulated, and new windows and a new furnace and boiler room were installed.

A corrections officer option, certified by the Michigan Department of Corrections, was added to the college's criminal justice program in fall 1987. Suomi was one of only 18 Michigan colleges to offer the corrections officer program at that time.

An Equestrian Club, with 30 female members, was the college's largest student organization in the 1987-88 academic year. Club members met four days a week, two hours per day, and rode as long as the outdoor temperature was at least seven degrees. Lu Griffin ('89) is pictured.

Graduate Vang Yee Leng Lee, a refugee from Laos, was a recipient of Suomi's Sisu Award for perseverance.

The tensions of the Arabian Gulf were far from the mind of graduate Seema Ingle of Bahrain.

1987 Commencement. The Paavo Nurmi Center was packed with graduates, their families and friends.

1988

In fall 1988 degree programs in medical records technology and automotive services management were begun, the eighth and ninth academic programs added to the school's curriculum since 1982.

Hikaru Yamamoto, a businessman in Chigasaki, Japan, began recruiting Japanese students to Suomi College in 1988, and continues to do so today. There are hundreds of Suomi and Finlandia University alumni in Japan.

1980s Japanese student Kaoru Inoue.

Student life in the 1980s.

1989

Dr. Robert Ubbelohde, who became president of the college in 1990, began as dean of faculty in March 1989. "Ubbelohde's arrival sparked a blaze of changes that one faculty member calls 'revolutionary, necessary, and exciting.'" (March 1989 *Bridge* 1)

Robert Ubbelohde in 1988.

Ubbelohde completed a bachelor's in philosophy and a master's and doctorate in education at the University of Wisconsin, and studied educational administration at Harvard University. Prior to his position at Suomi, he managed a department at the Aid Association for Lutherans and held university and grade school teaching positions.

"I would really love to be a college president," Ubbelohde says in the March 1989 *Bridge* article. "Where, when, I don't know. I don't have a timetable. I don't have a place in mind. I'm assuming that place is still out there." (4)

The residents of the Mickelsen House dormitory in 1989. The girls took part in a pilot living/learning program to foster skills in group decision-making, conflict resolution, and community building. Instructor Vicky Koskinen, back row, far left, initiated the pilot as part of a 1980s campus-wide initiative to instill within students ethical decision-making skills.

Associate professor of history and social sciences Dan Maki is interviewed by Finnish TV producer Lauri Niemelä in 1989. Niemala produced a documentary about Suomi College and the Copper Country that was aired on Finnish national television in July 1989. Maki retired in spring 2012 following 40 years of service to the college.

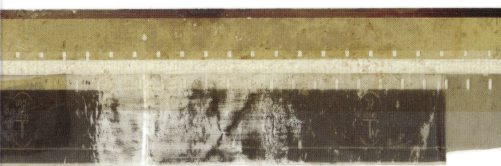

Residents of Old Main in the 1980s.

While Ubbelohde recognized that an educational institution could not be run exactly like a business, he believed that certain aspects—budgets and recognizing that a college offered a "product"—were best operated on business model.

He felt that key to the survival of private colleges like Suomi was the ability to quickly adapt to a changing world. A college "must run efficiently while maintaining or increasing quality," he says in the March 1989 *Bridge*, adding that with fierce competition among colleges for declining numbers of students, colleges must market themselves. "We now know we sell a product—we sell a successful career or future to people." (4)

With faculty input, he began a major reorganization of academic programs into four divisions, which took effect in fall 1989. By separating the college into divisions, Ubbelohde said, it will be better able to differentiate between students with divergent goals. He set a long-range student enrollment goal of 750 by 1994.

1990

Ralph Jalkanen retired from the college presidency effective August 1, 1990. Sidney Rand was named interim president while a search was conducted for a new president.

Ellwood Mattson, chairman of the board of trustees, says in the June 1990 *Bridge*, "We all have the highest regard for Ralph. … He is a legend in his own time. The names 'Ralph Jalkanen' and 'Suomi' are synonymous." (2)

Andrew Wisti, a member of the board's executive committee, added, "Suomi College wouldn't be in existence today if it weren't for Ralph Jalkanen. The college was ready to close when he became president, and it didn't because of him." (2)

Under Jalkanen's tenure, college enrollment tripled, financial support increased substantially, and five buildings were constructed: the Student Center (Mannerheim Hall) in 1965, Wargelin Hall in 1966, the Paavo Nurmi Center in 1969, Finlandia Hall in 1984, and the Finnish American Heritage Center in 1990. Also a milestone was North Central Association accreditation in 1969.

Jalkanen was awarded honorary doctoral degrees from three institutions, and the president of Finland bestowed upon him Finland's highest honor, The Order of the Lion, Commander's Medal. He was an author, a speaker, and the editor of several collections of essays about the Suomi Synod and the Finns in North America.

"Working for Suomi College wasn't a job," Jalkanen said. "It was a calling. … It was something special, something very human. To give oneself to a cause which is beyond ourselves is really the essence of life." (June 1990 *Bridge* 2)

On a humorous note, responding to a comment that the name of Suomi College is often mispronounced, Jalkanen said, "I never cared how they pronounced the name as long as they spelled it right on the check." (2)

Winter fun in the 1980s.

In 1990 Church of Finland bishop Rev. Paavo Kortekangas participated in the 100th anniversary of the Suomi Synod and FinnFest USA '90, which were both hosted by the college.

(L to R): Eric Edgren, Diane Weitzel, Steve Wilson, Ron Immonen, Phyllis Nemec, Lorri Barnes, Sue Knutson, Brent Cruea

Students perform the play "Li'l Abner" in 1988.

At a banquet in October 1990 more than 300 community leaders, politicians, educators, and friends honored Ralph and Pearl Jalkanen for their 30 years of service to the college and the community.

The Jalkanens in 1976.

Interim college president Sidney Rand was president of St. Olaf College in Northfield, Minnesota, for 17 years and a former U. S. ambassador to Norway.

The Finnish American Heritage Center was dedicated July 29, 1990, the final day of FinnFest USA '90. It was funded through a federal loan and gifts to the three-year "Mission of Hope" fundraising campaign, which by September 1990 had raised cash and pledges totaling $7.3 million.

Today, the building houses a community hall, the Finnish American Historical Archive, the Finlandia University Gallery, and the offices of the *Finnish American Reporter*. The building was designed by the Minnesota architecture firm of Eino (Jerry) Jyring and constructed by Yalmer Mattila Contracting, Inc.

Suomi College hosted FinnFest USA '90 in summer 1990.

"Thousands of Finns from nearly 50 states and two continents sojourned to Suomi to celebrate their heritage at FinnFest USA '90. The burgeoning crowds on opening day promised success. The enchanted crowds afterward affirmed the festival for future years. All in all, as flags fluttered in the breeze and the sound of song and dance carried over the campus, the four-day festival made memories for a lifetime. One woman said, 'This is the best time I've ever had in my life.' She was one of more than 5,000 who enjoyed the pageantry of the second FinnFest Suomi has hosted." (September 1990 *Bridge* 3)

FinnFest USA '90 activities.

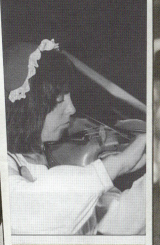

In 1993, the college hosted its first Summer Arts Festival, which was presented annually for several years.

CHAPTER NINE

1991-2007: A New Name, A New Model for Success

Robert and Susan Ubbelohde in 2007.
Photo by Adam Johnson.

While the years 1960 to 1990 were marked by remarkable growth—in giving, enrollment, and the physical plant—the three-decade period also left the college with long term debt of millions of dollars. The college continues to struggle under this burden.

Among the milestones during Robert Ubbelohde's presidency are the transition of Suomi College to a four-year university, a controversial name change, and the return of intercollegiate athletics. Capital improvements included renovation and expansion of the Sulo and Aileen Maki Library, construction of the Chapel of St. Matthew, major upgrades to campus technology, and the purchase, renovation, and opening of the Lily I. Jutila Center for Global Design and Business. Student enrollment increased and student retention saw annual improvements.

In 1991 the Old Main historical marker was acquired through the Michigan Bureau of History.

1991

On July 1, 1991, Ubbelohde assumed the presidency of Suomi College. Immediately, he engaged both on- and off-campus stakeholders in comprehensive strategic planning. "We went to Finland; we listened to alumni; we listened to everybody. There was open discussion about whether we should maintain the Finnish and Lutheran identities of the college," Ubbelohde recalls in the spring 2007 *Bridge*. (12)

"When I came here enrollment was dropping 8% a year," Ubbelohde notes. "As planning for the future began, the major questions were 'Do we try to save the college?' or 'Do we close it?' Once we decided to try to save it, the first direction from the board was to make it a viable two-year institution. And although attempts were then made to survive as a two-year college, they didn't succeed." (12)

Eventually, it was concluded that Suomi College become a niche, baccalaureate degree-granting institution.

The college adopted a new logo in 1991. Each of its five symbols represents a vital aspect of Suomi's educational mission: commitment to teaching and learning, educational opportunity for students, Finnish heritage, the Lutheran church, and the local community.

In the summer 1991 *Bridge* Ubbelohde shared many of the principles that would guide his 16-year tenure as president. (4-6)

Suomi as a college of opportunity. "We want to be an affordable, private option that concentrates on teaching. … While programs have been designed to serve the … top and bottom quartiles in our schools, the group in the middle has become the forgotten majority. The vast majority of these students have potential which can be unlocked by personalized, caring, creative and exciting teaching. It is this forgotten majority to which I want Suomi College to reach out."

A lively place for learning. "What a good teacher can do is bring learning alive. … Thus, the philosopher Whitehead suggested, the university serves to bring inert ideas or information alive through the coming together of young and old in the 'imaginative consideration of learning.' This is what I mean by Suomi being a 'lively' place."

Sound learning and quality. "It reflects my belief that we can always improve on what we are doing. … My emphasis on quality comes in part from this striving for perfection, continuing to improve what one is about … It also comes from the fact that I believe we need to provide students with a quality education."

Finnish-American heritage. "We need to focus our mission with regard to our Finnish-American heritage. … We need to find learning opportunities to engage third and fourth generation Finnish Americans … We also need to preserve … the artifacts and documents which comprise our archives … We need to find ways to include our Finnish heritage in literature, art, religion, philosophy, business, and other courses."

On an "alternate spring break" in 1991, students participated in a Habitat for Humanity home-building project in St. Louis, Missouri.

Global awareness in students and staff. "Our country is already competing and/or working cooperatively in an international environment. We need to prepare our students to participate in this environment. … There is much in our heritage as well as in our contemporary experience to urge us to think internationally."

A college of the church. " … it is a recognition of the religious faith of our Finnish immigrant founders. It is also a recognition … that we are a college of the Evangelical Lutheran Church in America. … I think we can affirm our faith without excluding people of other faiths. Lutherans have, in my experience, had a deep commitment to open dialogue and free inquiry."

The liberal arts. "The goal of liberal arts is, I believe, to teach people how to think critically and to open up their ability to think creatively. If this is done well it will lead to learners who value life-long learning."

During his first 18 months as president, Ubbelohde continued college restructuring with the aim of reducing costs through efficiency, while preserving quality, drawing on the "four Ps of marketing"—product, price, place, and promotion—plus a fifth "P," people.

For example, the budgets of the president's and development offices were reduced by more than 40 percent, yet in fiscal year 1991-92 private gifts and grants increased 39 percent.

"That's just one example of focusing and becoming more efficient," Ubbelohde says in the summer 1992 *Bridge*. "We must recognize that we are both an academic institution and a business." (6)

The existing "deployed" admissions program, in which recruiters worked from their homes in Michigan, Wisconsin, and Minnesota, was replaced with a more cost-efficient in-house recruitment model in which admissions counselors work from offices on campus, but travel more extensively. Another recruitment shift was from mass mailings to a more targeted approach and increased telemarketing. The moves saved $250,000 annually.

The Suomi College choir appeared on "CBS This Morning" January 11, 1991, singing in Finnish the television program's theme song, "Oh, What a Beautiful Morning." The performance, directed by Melvin Kangas, was taped outside of Finlandia Hall.

Ubbelohde's installation as president was celebrated September 27, 1991, with a ceremony, dinner, and dance at the Paavo Nurmi Center.

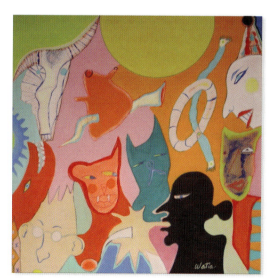

Watia's painting "There is always a clown around."

The first Contemporary Finnish American Artist Series exhibition, hosted annually at the Finlandia University Gallery since 1991, featured the paintings of artist Tarmo Watia. In 2008 Watia donated to the gallery's permanent collection 48 small, mixed-media drawings and paintings.

Hundreds of people attended the 28th annual Suomi College Smorgasbord in March 1992. Pictured are some of the event volunteers.

The academic area, which had been restructured into four departments when Ubbelohde was dean of faculty, saw more changes. The number of academic programs was scaled back and several faculty members were laid off. "Good education is labor intensive and any attempt to become more efficient usually includes looking at staff reductions," Ubbelohde says in the summer 1992 *Bridge*. (6)

All faculty and staff salaries were frozen, and for the first time employees began paying a portion of their health care insurance premiums. "I appreciate the support of faculty and staff to consider benefit adjustments to reduce the number of layoffs," Ubbelohde said. (Summer 1992 *Bridge* 6)

Finland's ambassador to the U. S., Jukka Valtasaari, delivered the commencement address May 5, 1991. "One hundred years ago, the language and culture, and people of Finland, were under threat. The name Suomi, which the college founders adopted, reflects the moral support they wished to offer their jeopardized homeland," Valtasaari said. (Summer 1991 *Bridge* 3)

In October 1991 Ubbelohde embarked on the first of more than 50 trips to Finland to develop networks of cooperation and personal relationships with Finnish educators and government and Church of Finland leaders. As Suomi's first non-Finnish president, Ubbelohde was sometimes asked if, as a non-Finn, he had to work harder to maintain the college's Finnish roots. "They say converts to a religion are always more active. I hope that's the case with heritage … We need our cultural mooring to bring a sense of wholeness to the education we offer." (Spring 2007 *Bridge* 10)

"I'm very happy about the sustained attention we've received from leaders and institutions in Finland," Ubbelohde reflects in the spring 2007 *Bridge*. "They're synergistic relationships in which we can help them, and they us." (15)

1992

In the summer 1992 *Bridge* Ubbelohde invites readers to take a tour of the future Suomi campus. "The year 2000 is eight years away. Suomi will begin its second century … Part of my job is to look ahead, envision the future, and then help guide the institution to that future."

"As I see it, Suomi has two choices: it can prosper and remain a lively place for sound learning, or it can slowly fade away … The future everyone at Suomi is working toward is the former."

Retired Lutheran Church in America bishop Nelson W. Trout traveled from Los Angeles to deliver the 1992 commencement address, May 3. "In a rousing and powerful speech, the retired Bishop Trout moved many of the 1,000 people at commencement to tears … and at the end, to their feet when he received a standing ovation." (Summer 1992 Bridge 4)

Soren Schmidt (left) and college chaplain Michael Martin. Schmidt, a 1994 Suomi liberal arts graduate, helped lead a weekly dormitory discussion group during the 1993-94 academic year with the theme, "Christianity in the 90s." "It's always easy to concentrate on sports and other purely recreational activities when you're scheduling programs for the dorm," Schmidt says in the March 1994 Bridge. "But I felt we also needed something that might help us answer questions about our faith and our personal values. … something to help us find direction for the future." (6) Schmidt has been university chaplain at Finlandia since 2009.

"As I begin my walk, I stop into the newly constructed academic center that connects Nikander and Wargelin halls. … I walk over to the new chapel on campus, a replica of an old Finnish church. … I make a quick trip to the Finnish American Heritage Center to discuss with the archivist plans for an addition to the archive. … After several hours of walking and talking, I return to the main administrative offices … in the refurbished Old Main. … Back at my own desk, I reflect on the list of 300 graduates who participated in commencement ceremonies this past spring. … Sometime before lunch, my mail arrives and in it is the latest issue of 'U.S. News and World Report.' The magazine contains the list of 'Best Buys' in higher education. Could it really be that Suomi is listed in the top 10?"

"As I see it, this is an achievable future for Suomi College," Ubbelohde concludes. " … Many difficult decisions must be made along the way, but with your continued support we can get there together." (7)

1994

In 1994 the college board "approved in principal" a proposal to reposition Suomi College as a four-year, niche university.

Bob and Susan Ubbelohde share a dance at a college-hosted Country and Western Show in the 1990s.

In the 1990s a Kellogg Foundation grant funded the installation of a distance learning system—video monitors, cameras, and other equipment—which linked a classroom in Nikander Hall with the Keweenaw Bay Tribal Center outreach classroom in Baraga, as well as with the distance learning classroom at the Regional Educational Media Center (REMC), Hancock. Longtime college dean Art Puotinen is pictured at the far left.

As part of the college's English as a Second Language program, in summer 1994 the program "Big Sky Classroom" introduced 14 Japanese students to life in the U.S. with 10 days of travel in the Southwest. The "traveling classroom" was conceived and directed by instructor Edith Wiard. When the students arrived at Suomi, three days of intensive classroom lessons were followed by a two-night hiking trip at Tahquamenon Falls. The "Big Sky Classroom" garnered national and international media attention in the *New York Times* and the *Tokyo Times*. (11)

1995

As Ubbelohde became acquainted with Finns and Finnish institutions, he learned of the Finnish model for sustainable economic development, in which major economic and government sectors cooperate to bring about business generation and growth. Finnish educational institutions play a central role in this process.

"Finland has found workable methods for cooperation between business (especially small business in rural areas) and education," Ubbelohde wrote from Finland in February 1995. "While eight faculty (working without pay) spend the summer working out the plan to implement design education curricula in fabric, ceramic, product ... and visual communication design, I am in Finland to finalize direct partnerships with Finnish design institutions. We believe we have found a unique niche for Suomi College ..." (Spring/summer 1995 *Bridge* 2)

There are many good reasons to partner with Finnish organizations and institutions, Ubbelohde notes in the summer 2003 *Bridge*. "First, our students do and will live in a global society. ... In addition, it is increasing both interest in and connections to Finland among a growing number of young people who will provide leadership within the Finnish American community in future years. ... There is [also] what might be called a symbiotic ... or 'networked' relationship between Finland, Finlandia, Finnish corporations and organizations, and the Finnish American community" (2)

A 1995 gift of $1 million from Aileen (Hill) Maki of LaJolla, California, in memory of her late husband, Sulo, funded the renovation and expansion of the library, which resulted in an increase in square footage from 6,300 to 12,100. Groundbreaking was in August 1995, renovations were completed in April 1996, and the new library was dedicated September 26, 1997. Aileen Maki was presented with the Suomi Lion Award in 1995 and an honorary doctorate in 1996.

Gloria Jackson, college trustee and Finnish Council in America member, in 1996. Jackson's interest in her own genealogy led to the establishment in 1996 of the Bill and Gloria Jackson Family History Center at the Finnish American Historical Archive. Funded by Jackson and others, the history center includes a comprehensive collection of genealogical records and resources from Finland, Sweden, the U.S., and around the world.

In April 1995 the college board approved bachelor degree programs in fine art and design and business administration, to be offered through the International School of Art & Design (ISAD) and the International School of Business (ISB), both established in 1996. The degree programs encourage an entrepreneurial approach to life and learning and pivot on practical internships with local businesses and organizations and partnerships with colleges and universities in Finland.

In the fall 1995 *Bridge* Ubbelohde reflects that Suomi's current plans for the future build on ideas set forth by V. K. Nikander in the college's 1946 jubilee year publication, such as Nikander's bold vision of Suomi College as a four-year college and curriculum development that would incorporate the teaching of Finnish folk arts and crafts.

"As we now prepare for our 100th anniversary in 1996, we approach our centennial with plans to become a baccalaureate degree-granting institution with majors based in Finnish folk arts and crafts," Ubbelohde says. "Our plans are to be the only institution in the United States offering Finnish-based design education. … In some ways then, we have 'gone back to the future' in extending Nikander's ideas." (2)

In a competition for the design of a logo and theme for the Suomi College Centennial, Melanie Solka designed the winning image above, which was used throughout the centennial year. Joe Tormala, then-director of security at the college, proposed the centennial theme, "Celebrating 100 years of opportunity and excellence."

1996

On February 26, 1996, Suomi College was granted accreditation as a baccalaureate degree-granting institution by the North Central Association Higher Learning Commission, and subsequently by additional state and national accrediting bodies.

Jaakko Laajava, ambassador of Finland to the United States, presented the commencement address April 28, 1996.

In fall 1996 a pre-physical therapist assistant (PTA) program began, and in fall 1997 the PTA associate degree program enrolled its first class. The PTA program has been continuously accredited by the Commission on Accreditation of Physical Therapy Education (CAPTE) since 1998. Through 2013, 199 students have successfully completed the program.

Gloria Jackson was elected chairman of the Suomi College Board of Trustees in fall 1996, the first woman to fill that office. Jackson began her service on the board in 1987. She was chair from 1997 until 2003, then secretary until early 2011, then chair again until her unexpected death in 2011. At April 2003 commencement Jackson was awarded an honorary doctor of humane letters.

A new college logo was introduced in conjunction with centennial year celebrations. "The Christian symbolism of the triangle (trinity), circle (eternity/never-ending existence), and square (earth/earthly existence) underscores the college's Lutheran heritage." (June 1996 Bridge 1)

Special guests in attendance at the August 1996 groundbreaking for the Chapel of St. Matthew were Evangelical Lutheran Church of Finland archbishop John Vikström, ELCA bishop H. George Anderson, ELCA Northern Great Lakes Synod bishop Dale Skogman, Matti Parjanen, vice rector, University of Tampere, and former Suomi College president Raymond Wargelin. Ubbelohde is pictured at far right.

Traditional Finnish graduation caps, handmade replicas of those worn by early Suomi College students, were donned by graduates and faculty for April 28, 1996, centennial year commencement. Image used with permission of the Daily Mining Gazette.

In conjunction with 1996 centennial celebrations, Suomi College: A Century of Opportunity, a 93-page photo album, was published by the college.

Summer 1996 centennial activities included a college history exhibit at the Finnish American Heritage Center and an all-school reunion in July. A Suomi College Heritage Celebration, August 2 to August 4, included groundbreaking ceremonies for library expansion and the Chapel of St. Matthew, the grand opening of the Family History Center, genealogy workshops, a traditional Finnish dinner prepared by student-chefs from the Porvoo Institute of Travel and Tourism, and a concert by the Finnish-American brass septet, "Ameriikan Poijat." On August 10 Riita Maria Uosukainen, Finland's speaker of the parliament, visited campus, and a Community Centennial Celebration Dinner was hosted September 27, at which the college was presented with a "Special Tribute" from the state of Michigan in honor of the college's centennial year.

1997

In fall 1997 the PTA program began classes in a rented building on Quincy Street, which had previously housed a physical therapy clinic, across from the Finnish American Heritage Center. "We had many discussions about where the program would be located," says longtime PTA program chair Cam Williams in the winter 1997 *Bridge*. "This place became available at the right time … [It's] just about perfect." (3)

The Finlandia University Community Partners advisory board was established in 1997. The group of community leaders, business people, and educators meets on campus two or three times each year to learn about university accomplishments, challenges, and future plans, and to share their thoughts and ideas with university administration.

In January 1997 a lab equipped with 24 computers, the latest software, laser printers, and Internet access was opened on the second floor of Nikander Hall. The lab was funded by emeritus trustee Willard Cohodas and his wife, Lois, in memory of Willard Cohodas's parents.

In April 1997 the library occupied its new, larger space and the International School of Art & Design celebrated the opening of remodeled facilities in Nikander Hall, which included a visual communications lab and art studios.

1998

On March 6, 1998, Ubbelohde received the Arts and Letters Award from the New York Metropolitan Chapter of the Finlandia Foundation in recognition of his leadership in enhancing the college's academic excellence and cultural exchange with Finland and Finnish universities, and for establishing a full baccalaureate degree program at Suomi.

A reunion of seminary faculty, staff, students, and friends took place April 24 to April 26, 1998, marking the 40th anniversary of the 1958 separation of the Suomi Theological Seminary from the college. Among attendees were former college presidents David Halkola and Raymond Wargelin.

Following a site visit in January, on May 6, 1998, the PTA program was granted initial accreditation by the Commission on Accreditation in Physical Therapy Education (CAPTE). A grant from the Retirement Research Foundation of Chicago supported the PTA program in its early years.

In summer 1998 Robert Winter of Lenoir-Rhyne College, North Carolina, visited Suomi as part of a faculty exchange program funded in part by a $40,000 grant from the Lutheran Brotherhood to incorporate a liturgical design component in the art and design curriculum. Also part of the exchange, in September 1998 art and design faculty member Phyllis (Fredendall) McIntyre visited Lenoir-Rhyne and displayed her fiber arts work there.

In August 1998 the college received notification that a three-year $275,894 grant from the U.S. Department of Education Fund for the Improvement of Post-secondary Education (FIPSE) was funded. The grant provided financial support for the development and implementation of the International School of Art & Design's business-based, Finnish-inspired fine art and design curriculum.

Pictured are (left to right): John Sederholm, Denise Vandeville, and Jon Brookhouse.

Suomi art and design students Denise Vandeville ('01), John Sederholm, and Susan Hartfield, with Jon Brookhouse, ISAD ceramics instructor and dean, created a relief sculpture for the entrance canopy at Gloria Dei Lutheran Church, Hancock. The series of 60 ceramic tiles, dedicated August 30, 1998, represents the biblical passage "Come to me, all who labor and are heavy laden, and I will give you rest." (Matthew 11:28)

In August 1998 the North Central Association authorized Suomi College to offer a B.A. in Liberal Studies: Rural Human Services, which started in fall 1998. A two-year human services associate degree had been established at the college in the 1970s.

In fall 1998 a dual business/criminal justice B.B.A. degree program was begun, and the college's distance learning classroom at the Keweenaw Bay Indian Community, Baraga, was reopened with grant support from the Elizabeth E. Kennedy Fund and the Ford Motor Company.

In winter 1998 it was announced that the "Nurturing a Legacy of Opportunity" capital campaign, which began its "quiet phase" in June 1994 and was scheduled for completion in June 2000, had reached 82% of its $18.7 million goal. The largest capital campaign undertaken by the college up to that time, it was launched to meet the goals of transforming Suomi College into a baccalaureate degree-granting institution of higher learning, and in particular to raise funds to support plant and program growth and provide additional student scholarships, among other related projects.

Above: President Ubbelohde takes a brief break outside the Hoover Center.

Top left: A student talks with Mary Tormala, director of the Rural Human Services B.A. degree program, in the 1990s.

Bottom left: The first class of PTA graduates received their diplomas April 27, 1998.

1999

After a 14-year absence, in fall 1999 the college reintroduced intercollegiate athletics, starting with men's and women's basketball. Today, Finlandia student-athletes compete in 13 men's and women's NCAA Division III sports.

"At one point, I said that it would be over my dead body that we'd bring athletics back," Ubbelohde says in the spring 2007 *Bridge*. (15) He became convinced, however, that the opportunity to participate in intercollegiate sports would persuade more area youth to attend college in the Upper Peninsula.

"Hail to thee, Finlandia." In September 1999 the board of trustees voted overwhelmingly to change the name of Suomi to Finlandia University—pending favorable outcome of inquiries regarding state of Michigan requirements for the use of "university." The new name took effect July 1, 2000.

In spring 1999 the first B.B.A. degrees were awarded to 11 graduates.

The Ubbelohdes with the 1999 Sibelius Academy musicians.

The first annual Sibelius Academy Music Festival was July 28 to 31, 1999. Eight musicians from Helsinki's prestigious music academy performed concerts in Hancock, Pelkie, and Eagle Harbor, Michigan; Wheaton, Illinois; New Marlborough, Massachusetts; and Stamford, N.Y. The concert series has continued annually since. Pictured is the string quartet Touché at Holy Cross Lutheran Church, Wheaton, in 1999.

The name change decision was informed by two surveys, in particular. Of the 10,000 potential students who responded to one, the name Finlandia was preferred 2:1 over Suomi. The results were evenly split in a similar survey of alumni, faculty, and staff.

"The new name—Finlandia—reaffirms our connection to Finland …" says board chairman Gloria Jackson in the winter 1999 *Bridge*. "As we enter a new millennium, we need to look forward. … It is time to take [our] wonderful heritage and offer it to students across the country and around the world. The name Finlandia is immediately recognized as … connected to Finland … [It] will let potential students know exactly what the College is …" (3)

But the vote was not an easy one for some trustees. "As a native Finn, one of eight on the board, I'm torn," said Tiimo Siimes. "If I vote with my heart, it's Suomi. If I vote with my head, it's Finlandia. I think this time, I prefer my head." (3)

In 1999 North Wind Books was gifted to the university by Peter and Patricia Van Pelt of Eagle Harbor, Michigan. Susan Ubbelohde was manager of the bookstore for eight years, until President Ubbelohde's retirement in 2007. "When Robert asked me to help him realize the vision for North Wind Books I wasn't looking for anything else to do, but I've found that it's really nice to do something on campus that is separate from my role as the president's wife," she says in the spring 2007 Bridge. (7) In 2005, an addition to North Wind Books, which is located adjacent to the Finnish American Heritage Center, added textbook sales and storage space.

2000

The first Chapel of St. Matthew worship service was conducted by university chaplain Bucky Brown-Beach on February 15, 2000. The two-story, 3,800-square-foot chapel, designed by architect John Haro, is modeled after the simple churches built by early Finnish immigrants to the Copper Country. It was funded by a grant from the Siebert Lutheran Foundation, donations from parishioners of the Evangelical Lutheran Church of Finland, and gifts from individual donors.

In April 2000 the North Central Association conducted a comprehensive site visit, recommending renewal of college accreditation for a period of seven years, and approving B.A. in Liberal Studies programs in general studies and Great Books, Great Voices, which both began in fall 2000.

Among the nearly 100 degrees awarded at commencement April 28, 2000, 14 were baccalaureate degrees in art and design, business administration, and liberal studies.

The chapel was dedicated July 17, 2000, with the archbishop of Finland, Jukka Paarma, officiating, assisted by Thomas Skrenes, bishop of the ELCA Northern Great Lakes Synod, Antti Lepisto, president of the ELCA Suomi Special Interest Conference, and local clergy. "Back in the early days, Bob was determined that Finlandia needed a chapel," recalls university trustee Sam Benedict in the spring 2007 Bridge. "He would often say, 'What's a Lutheran school without a chapel?' Bob had a vision, stuck with it, and never lost faith or gave up hope." (18)

On July 1, 2000, Suomi College became Finlandia University.

In fall 2000, athletics programs in men's hockey, women's volleyball, and men's and women's cross country running began.

At a ceremony October 24, 2000, in Hancock, Finland's ambassador to the U.S., Jaakko Laajava, presented to Ubbelohde the Cross of the Order of the Finnish Lion, First Class—one of the highest honors awarded by the Finnish government—in recognition of Ubbelohde's success in enhancing Finlandia University, its programs, and its links to Finland.

Finland prime minister Paavo Lipponen delivered the April 28, 2000, commencement address and received an honorary doctor of laws degree. Lipponen is pictured following commencement, at a local elementary school, and with Ubbelohde and Yalmer Mattila.

In January 2000 *The Finnish American Reporter* (FAR) published its first issue from the campus of Suomi College. In 1999 the Superior, Wisconsin-based Työmies Society gifted the FAR and substantial assets to the college. The inaugural issue of the FAR was distributed at FinnFest 1986 in Berkley, California.

"For the Työmies Society to give the paper to Suomi College is a very important symbol of the healing of Finnish America," says Jim Kurtti, current editor of the FAR, in the fall 2005 *Bridge*. "In 1913, the Työmies Society and its publications were literally 'run out of town' as tensions among striking workers and the mining industry reached a boiling point." (17)

Today, the monthly English-language publication has a growing circulation of 3,600 with readers in all 50 states, in Canada, and on five continents. The FAR provides a forum for all points of view within the Finnish-American community and is without political or religious affiliation.

The first B.F.A. graduating class, April 2000. Clockwise from bottom, left: Tina Erickson, Lorrie Matheson Nesbitt, Angela Smith, and Judy Puotinen.

The first B.A. in Liberal Studies: Rural Human Services graduating class, April 2000. Clockwise from bottom, left: Karen Clogston, Michelle Hanna, Sarah Nankee, Calvin Harris, Lisa Peterson, Marie Salo Posio, Amy Sturma, and program director Mary Tormala.

"Dr. Tormala is tough, task oriented, and persistent at times, but everything she does is in the interest in developing her students and urging them to grow," said Shelley Sivonen, Class of 2001 valedictorian and one of 14 to be awarded a B.A. in human services that year. (Spring 2001 *Bridge* 7)

2001

In the winter 2001 *Bridge* Ubbelohde summarizes notable changes of the preceding decade. "Ten years later, our enrollment is up for the third straight year and we have raised academic standards—our ACT scores increased 5.8 percent this fall continuing three years of increase. … Students enjoy the new library facility, the chapel, the new art and design building, as well as a computer to student ratio of 5:1. We have three Finnish nationals on the faculty and staff … Our chaplain is an active member of the community both leading curricular change and our new 'servant leadership' program. … We have nine Ph.D.s on staff. … We are completing a half-million dollar project to upgrade technology, which includes wiring and thereby networking of all computers on campus … [however] Some things do not change. Over 80 percent of students are the first in their families to attend college and over 90 percent require financial assistance … We serve a large percentage of foreign and minority students, giving us great diversity. We continue our tradition of being a school of educational opportunity." (2)

The sisters of Becky (Lasanen) Swykert (far left, a 2001 associate degree in nursing alumna) completed Finlandia's A.D.N. program in 2005, which was the final graduating class. Rachel, Katie, and Norah Lasanen are also pictured.

"Heikki Jylhä-Vuorio, visiting professor from the Kuopio (Finland) Academy of Design and ISAD dean from 2001 to 2005, led the design and implementation of Finlandia's B.F.A. program.

On October 12, 2001, students marked the tragedy of September 11, 2001, with a special worship service and the dedication of a memorial honoring the victims. The memorial was funded through the leadership of the Business Club, which also collected food and monetary donations to send to the victims.

The university hosted a public forum October 20, 2001, at the Finnish American Heritage Center to encourage further conversation in the wake of the September terrorist attacks. Houghton County residents from the United Arab Emirates, Iran, Sudan, and other places around the world gave brief presentations.

2001-02 resident assistants (left to right): front row: Bill Melchiori, Mike O'Donnell, Scott Raisanen; back: Iloni Kotila, Ginger Hay, Natalie Johnson, and residence life director Denise Whitaker.

On March 9, 2001, the Finlandia men's basketball team captured the National Small Colleges Athletic Association (NSCAA) championship, finishing the season with a 17-14 record. Coach Art Van Damme ('70) was named NSCAA Coach of the Year. "[Winning] the national championship with a bunch of Yoopers, one Finnish guy, and a troll from down under the bridge—it was great," says team member and tournament MVP Mike O'Donnell in the spring 2001 *Bridge*. (12)

At the institution's first commencement as Finlandia University, April 29, 2001, 27 graduates were awarded baccalaureate degrees, and 44 received associate degrees. In recognition of their support of Finlandia's advancement, both Ubbelohde and Bart Stupak, U.S. Representative from Michigan's 1st congressional district, received awards from the Michigan Association of Independent Colleges and Universities.

2002

In July 2002 Ubbelohde was appointed honorary consul for the Upper Peninsula of Michigan by the Finnish Ministry of Foreign Affairs. He succeeded local television personality Carl Pellonpaa, who had reached Finland's mandatory retirement age.

"Consider the birch leaf," suggests an article announcing Finlandia's adoption of a new logo. "Our dedication to individual growth through 'academic excellence, spiritual growth and service' is represented by the fresh green birch leaf … As our students grow, we will grow and so it is with the birch." The current Finlandia Lions logo, also adopted in 2002, "symbolizes athletic prowess while still representing academics and the heritage and dignity of Finlandia University." (Winter 2002 *Bridge*)

2001-02 men's hockey.

In a spring 2002 exhibit of student art work B.F.A. graduate Becky Weeks ('03) was awarded Best of Show for her design and construction of the pictured costume, modeled by Melvin Kangas (right).

On a servant leadership trip May 1 to May 8, 2002, eleven students and four faculty members traveled to the Yucatan Peninsula, Mexico, to help build a school for the community of Puerto Morelos.

The 2002-03 women's volleyball team.

Author Parker Palmer was a campus mentor in fall 2002. "Good teaching cannot be reduced to technique," Palmer said. "Good teaching comes from the identity and integrity of the teacher." (Winter 2002 *Bridge* 11). Palmer's week-long visit was sponsored by Finlandia's Liberal Studies: Great Books/Great Voices B.A. program and a multi-year grant from the McGregor Fund, which presented opportunities for students and faculty to interact with contemporary scholars.

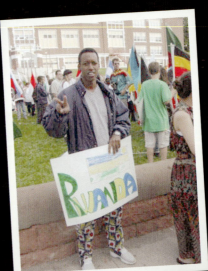

An international student from Rwanda, in the early 2000s.

Homemade Finnish prune tarts were served at the fall 2002 Alumni Banquet. Pictured are the bakers and banquet volunteers.

The rural human services bachelor of arts program required its majors to research a community non-profit agency, illustrate their findings on a triptych, and display them in a "poster session," at which campus community members could view the triptychs and ask questions of the student.

A student life Halloween party in October 2002.

The University Singers in October 2002.

After appearing November 4 to December 13, 2002, at the Finlandia University Gallery, in summer and fall 2003 the tenth annual Contemporary Finnish American Artist Series exhibit, "From the Beginning: Retrospective (1991-2001)," traveled to five art galleries in Finland. Pictured below are a few of the exhibit postcards.

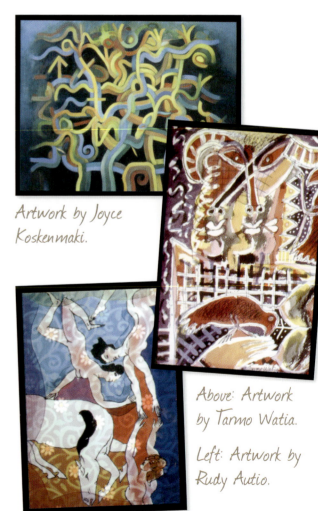

Artwork by Joyce Koskenmaki.

Above: Artwork by Tarmo Watia.

Left: Artwork by Rudy Autio.

In December 2002 a hand-crafted cross was fastened to the steeple of the Chapel of St. Matthew. Designed by Craig Fish ('02), the cross was the gift of Andrea McAleenan of Santa Monica, Calif., and Karen Richards of San Diego, in memory of their mother, 1934 Suomi graduate Elaine (Halmekangas) Hautala (1913-2000). In April 2010, McAleenan and Richards arranged permanent exterior lighting for the cross in remembrance of their father, Edward Henry Hautala (1914-2009).

2003

A program of study since 1983, in January 2003 Finlandia's nursing program completed its first step in becoming a four-year baccalaureate program with approval of the generic bachelor of science in nursing (B.S.N.) by the Michigan State Board of Nursing. With graduation of the final A.D.N. class in 2005, the transition to a four-year B.S.N. was complete. From 1985 to 2005 the A.D.N. program graduated 463 nurses. The first class of B.S.N. graduates was in 2007, and through 2013, 149 have successfully completed the four-year program.

Finland president Tarja Halonen at 2003 commencement. At the conclusion of her speech Halonen said, "It's good to have a friend, and you have a friend. You have me, and you have Finland." (Summer 2003 Bridge 2) A videotape of the commencement ceremonies was produced.

Class of 2003 Sampo Society inductees (left to right): Teresa Sayatovich, Bertha Rogers, Pearl Currey, Lillian Sederholm, and Michelle Hall.

In spring 2003 Finland president Tarja Halonen visited the Copper Country and delivered the April 27 Finlandia University commencement address. At an April 25 address to Class of 2003 baccalaureate graduates, Halonen was awarded an honorary doctor of humane letters. "It's easy to be for social justice without caring," said Ubbelohde, adding that for Halonen, "social justice is not an election theme to get elected. It comes from her heart and the depth of her soul. She cares about people …" (Summer 2003 *Bridge* 8)

Other distinguished guests at 2003 commencement were Jukka Valtasaari, ambassador of Finland to the U.S., and Jukka Leino, consul general of Finland in New York.

The International Alumni Board in June 2003 (left to right): John Stierna ('63), Ruth Stierna, Lois (Isaac) Seaton ('50), Charleen (Hewer) Ahola ('65), Scott Dickson ('58), Sylvia (Saari) Fleishman ('58), Jeanne (Wierimaa) Kemppainen ('59), Sigrid (Ojala) Bartelli ('38), Shirley (Miller) Kukkonen ('41), Norma (Mickelson) Nominelli ('51), Eve (Kangas) Lindsey ('62), Susan (Hegstrom) Stoor ('69), Louis Marchiol ('61), and Jan Wisniewski ('93). In summer 1999 the Suomi College National Alumni Board was re-established as the Finlandia University International Alumni Board.

Women's hockey team members help out at the Copper Country Humane Society, Chassell.

Laura Sayen (left) and Nicole Ross are the first recipients of the B.A. in Liberal Studies: Elementary Education. They received their diplomas April 27, 2003.

Fred Knoch ('09) paints a repurposed door.

2003-04 men's soccer.

Students in an Environmental Studies class during an overnight stay at the Lake Linden (Michigan) School Forest cabin.

In June 2003 Finlandia was accepted as a provisional member of the National Collegiate Athletic Association (NCAA) Division III, effective September 1, 2003. Eight varsity athletic programs were approved by the NCAA, increasing athletic programs from four to 12. Fall 2003 additions were men's and women's soccer and Nordic skiing, women's fast-pitch softball, and men's baseball.

"A new age of Finlandia Athletics is approaching sooner than anyone could have imagined," says athletic director Chris Salani in the spring 2003 *Bridge*. "We're at a lightening quick pace right now, and we all need to hang on to our hats." (6)

In fall 2003 a B.B.A. sports management concentration began, and the B.A. in Liberal Studies: Great Books, Great Voices became the inter-disciplinary B.A. in Liberal Studies: ACE (Arts, Culture & Environment).

Above: 2003-04 women's softball.

Left: Sara Sleik ('08) donates blood in the mid-2000s.

In the 2003-04 academic year Finlandia welcomed students from Japan, Finland, Turkey, Singapore, Canada, Rwanda, China, India, Romania, Nepal, Mexico, and Taiwan. Pictured are Japanese students Kiyo and Taka in 2003.

The Paavo Nurmi Center bowling alley was converted to a fitness center in 2003. Underutilization of the bowling alleys and the need for a more secure fitness area were among the reasons for the change. "So it's 'so long' to the noisy ball returns, the crashing of pins and the thunder of rolling balls. Say 'hello' to the grunting and grimacing that accompanies straining muscles, the rhythmic patter of aerobic workouts and the audible exhalation of people keeping their bodies fit." (Fall 2003 *Bridge* 8)

2004

On March 3, 2004, the women's basketball team captured the USCAA National Basketball Championship in Portland, Maine, in an overtime defeat of Arkansas Baptist College, 78-77. Student-athlete Beth Koski ('04) was named 2004 All-American and Academic All-American; Jessica Koski ('05), 2004 Academic All-American; and Delsie Luokkala ('04), All-American Honorable Mention. Coach Steve Nordstrom was named USCAA Coach of the Year.

In the 2004-05 academic year Finlandia art and design students, with students at 12 design schools in China, Japan, Germany, the United Kingdom, Finland, and U.S., pursued a first-of-its-kind cross-cultural project called Global Design Solutions Network (GDSNet). "A global design approach entails a study of the cultural characteristics of design in a variety of countries," says ISAD dean Heikki Jylhä-Vurio in the fall 2004 *Bridge*. "The cultural context in which consumer products will be used has a great influence on the design of products." (12)

In fall 2004 the women's hockey program began and the team was accepted into the Northern Collegiate Hockey Association (NCHA). It was just the second collegiate women's hockey team in Michigan. Also in fall 2004, the men's hockey team was accepted into the Midwest Collegiate Hockey Association (MCHA).

"I continually ask myself, 'How did we win the National Championship,'" Coach Nordstrom writes in the summer 2004 *Bridge*. "I find there is more than one answer. First, the talent here when I took over this team two years ago. ... Second, the team had depth in all positions, and we believed in each member of the team. That confidence paid off ... Third, our four seniors were not going to let us lose; they were determined to end their careers as champions. Finally, the people at Finlandia made a big difference. They helped and supported this team at all times." (12)

Women's basketball senior Trista Wills "cuts the winning net" in March 2004 following the team's capture of that spring's USCAA National Basketball Championship in Portland, Maine.

In 2003-04 Finlandia launched a new website designed by art and design alumnus Mike Stockwell ('01). The same year, the website was awarded gold and bronze cyber-medals by HMR Publications Group.

Cross country runners in 2004.

Left: Students "make wood" for Little Brothers Friends of the Elderly in 2003-04.

Below: 2004-05 women's hockey.

Left: Arts, Culture & Environment (ACE) majors with Copper Country outdoorsman Bill Deephouse (left) in 2004.

Japanese Suomi College and Finlandia University alumni periodically meet for all-class reunions. Pictured is a May 2004 gathering in Takayama, Japan.

Longtime Japanese student recruiter Hikaru Yamamoto was presented with the Finlandia Lion Award in 2007.

Barry Lopez, award-winning author of Arctic Dreams and other non-fiction, was a campus mentor March 31 to April 6, 2004.

Pirjo Vaittinen, senior lecturer in Finnish pedagogy at the University of Tampere, was the first Fulbright Scholar hosted by Finlandia, and the first-ever Finnish national requested by a U.S. college to serve as a Scholar-in-Residence. Among other endeavors, during the 2004-05 academic year Vaittinen conducted an internet-based literature course, Contemporary Fiction From Finland, in which Finlandia students, community members, and University of Tampere students were enrolled. Vaittinen (left) is pictured with Anna Leppänen.

"An alumni birthday party was held last April (2004) honoring Nelma Kananen '35, Edward Hautala '47, and Rachel Hetico, '44. The celebration included accordion music as well as singing by Edward and his two daughters Andrea and Karen. Edward's daughters also sang the "Old Suomi March" and "Happy Birthday," which was sung 3 times for each honoree. Lunch and coffee were served to honor the alumni. These three alumni are part of the Florida Friends of Finlandia group. The group held several fund raisers recently, donating more than $4,000 to Finlandia University scholarship programs. The fund raising activities included a breakfast/raffle/bake sale and a Thanksgiving Dinner last fall." (Fall 2004 *Bridge* 19)

Friends and Alumni of Finlandia University was established in January 1979 by Ed Happa ('33) and a group of other college alumni and senior adults in the Lantana and Lake Worth, Florida, area.

Above: 2004-05 Nordic ski team.

Right: Class of 2004 graduates.

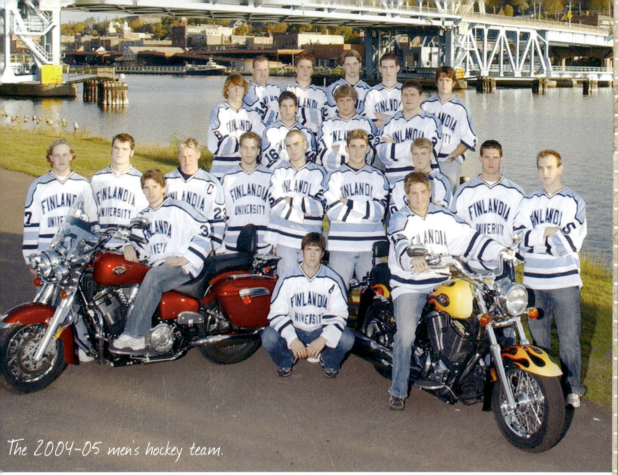

The 2004-05 men's hockey team.

Ubbelohde is pictured with athletic director Chris Salani.

In spring 2005 a 6,000 square foot addition to the Houghton County Ice Arena, Hancock, was completed, which includes 2,600 square-feet of dedicated space for Finlandia hockey programs. A men's locker room—with bath and shower facilities, lockers, a sauna, coaches' offices, and storage areas—was dedicated October 10, 2005. The addition was wholly funded by local community members.

Left: Ron and Sue Antila funded a hockey locker for the new men's locker room at the Houghton County Arena.

Hockey players check out the sauna in the new hockey locker room. Pictured are Joe Welgos (07), Mitch Tallent (08), and Luke Alberer (08).

2005

Finland ambassador to the U.S., Jukka Valtasaari (pictured at right with Carl Pellonpaa) presented the commencement address May 1, 2005. In 2007 Valtasaari said of Ubbelohde, "Bob brought the early history of Finnish emigration to North American back to Finland. Before he began his visits to Finland, this was something historical to which we didn't pay much attention. Bob appealed to our interest in our ancestors, told the story, and got our attention." (Spring 2007 *Bridge* 19)

By fall 2005 student enrollment had increased 65.2%, from 336 students in fall 1995 to 555 in fall 2005, accompanied by yearly improvements in student retention.

The Lily I. Jutila Center for Global Design and Business was dedicated September 23, 2005. "Of the more than 300 business incubators at institutions of higher learning in the United States, Finlandia's is one of a kind," says Ubbelohde in the winter 2005 *Bridge*, explaining that the two things that make the facilities unique are an art and design bachelor degree program embedded within a small business incubator, and the MTEC SmartZone adding entrepreneurial engineers to the mix. The Jutila Center is also home to the studios, classrooms, and offices of the International School of Art & Design.

Below: The summer 2004 Elderhostel program, "A Celebration of Finnish Culture," was particularly meaningful for participant Mirja Bishop, Los Angeles, California, who, in a journal of her experiences, wrote:

"My Finnish spirit has been rekindled and restored. I now have a clearer understanding of why my parents immigrated to Canada from Finland in 1929. I never realized how much my Finnish heritage had influenced my life." (Winter 2004 Bridge 26) Bishop is pictured in the pink t-shirt.

The 2004-05 Finlandia women's basketball team won the inaugural Association of Division III Independents Northeast II Regional Championship February 26, 2005, in Troy, New York, with a 58-49 win over New Jersey City University. Brooke Sirard (#30) was named tournament MVP.

Nursing students at Omega House hospice, Houghton, in fall 2005.

2005-06 men's baseball.

Riku F. Lion (Bill Melchiori, '04) and Jim Harden ('02), Finlandia director of security, march in the August FinnFest USA 2005 parade in Marquette, Michigan.

Phase One renovations to levels one, two, and three of the nine-floor Jutila Center, begun in July 2004, were completed in fall 2005. The extensive work was funded by grants from the U.S. Commerce Department Economic Development Administration (EDA) and the Michigan Economic Development Corporation (MEDC), matched by private donations, including a 2004 bequest of $3 million from the estate of Finnish American Lily I. Jutila. The building, formerly the Portage View Hospital, was purchased in 2001 from the city of Hancock—for one dollar.

"Two universities, two communities, and a number of community organizations had to cooperate and collaborate to make this a possibility," said Phil Musser, executive director of the Keweenaw Economic Development Alliance. " … I hope that you will look at this building and see our future. New companies, entrepreneurs home grown in the Copper Country, are … the lifeblood of our economy." (3)

Established in 1999 as the Business Innovation Center, Finlandia's Center for Global Design and Business (CGDB) encourages entrepreneurial activity in the Copper Country by providing assistance and resources to emerging small businesses. Since 2005, 71 businesses have leased suites in the center, several of them owned and operated by Finlandia art and design graduates. A 2005 Coleman Foundation grant added rapid prototyping equipment, services, and support.

Pictured are former Jutila Center director Joanne MacInnes (left) with Ubbelohde (center) and Michigan Technological University president Glen Mroz at the September 2005 Jutila Center dedication.

Lily I. Jutila.

2006

In January 2006 Rev. Dr. Philip Johnson was appointed Finlandia University campus pastor and assistant to the president. From August 2006 until June 2007, he also served as associate dean of Finlandia's Suomi College of Arts & Sciences.

Johnson, a pastor in the Evangelical Lutheran Church in America (ELCA), arrived at Finlandia with 23 years of church-related leadership experience. From 1999 to 2005 he was a professor and dean at the Mekane Yesus Theological Seminary and the Ethiopian Graduate School of Theology in Addis Ababa. He supervised the Nairobi Lutheran Parish of the Kenya Evangelical Lutheran Church from 1992 to 1996, and was associate pastor at Our Savior's Lutheran Church in Circle Pines, Minnesota, from 1988 to 1991.

Johnson earned his B.A. at Concordia College, Moorhead, Minnesota, and his M.Div. and Ph.D. at Luther Seminary, St. Paul, Minnesota. His spouse, René Johnson, is assistant professor of religion and philosophy and director of servant leadership at Finlandia.

"I'm one of the new kids on the block," writes Philip Johnson in the summer 2006 *Bridge*, noting that his transition from the Horn of Africa to the Upper Peninsula was relatively smooth. "I have found that whether in the 'Horn' or in Hancock, people are willing to make room for a full-blooded Norwegian, oddities and all." (12)

Neal, René, Philip, and Simon Johnson in 2007.

John Mackey ('06) with David Tiede following Baccalaureate on April 28, 2006.

Below: Class of 2006 elementary education graduates (left to right): Kristina Mechlin, Shanda Jacques, Scott LaBonte, Amanda Pasonen, and Kasey Engman.

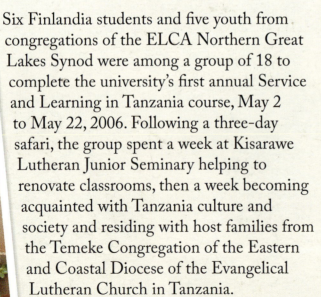

Six Finlandia students and five youth from congregations of the ELCA Northern Great Lakes Synod were among a group of 18 to complete the university's first annual Service and Learning in Tanzania course, May 2 to May 22, 2006. Following a three-day safari, the group spent a week at Kisarawe Lutheran Junior Seminary helping to renovate classrooms, then a week becoming acquainted with Tanzania culture and society and residing with host families from the Temeke Congregation of the Eastern and Coastal Diocese of the Evangelical Lutheran Church in Tanzania.

In a long-term campus improvement project that began in 2006, technological upgrades fully networked all campus buildings for high-speed data and voice communications through the installation of thousands of yards of exterior and interior multiple-strand fiber optic cables. By 2012 wireless Internet access was available campus-wide.

In fall 2006 the College of Professional Studies established an RN-to-BSN degree completion program, and the B.A. in Liberal Studies: ACE was designated an honors program.

On September 1, 2006, Finlandia became a full member of NCAA Division III, completing the four-year membership process a full year ahead of schedule. What does this mean for Finlandia athletics? asks an article in the winter 2006 *Bridge*. "In a word, credibility," says athletic director Chris Salani in the article, explaining that NCAA membership provides schools with similar missions and philosophies the opportunity to align themselves for athletic competition. Division III institutions place highest priority on the overall student-athlete experience and the successful completion of academic requirements. (9)

Fall 2006 student enrollment, at 587, was the highest in 19 years and up nearly 60% since the introduction of baccalaureate programs in fall 1996. More than 70% of 2006-07 students were from the Upper Peninsula, two-thirds were women, and nearly 160 lived on campus. Eighty students were from other states, and 20 international students hailed from Japan, Tanzania, France, and Canada. More than half declared College of Professional Studies majors, 17% were business majors, 14% were art and design majors, 10% majored in the arts and sciences.

International students at the 2006 Parade of Nations.

Students outside Finlandia Hall on Activities Day, August 29, 2006.

The student-run Reflection Gallery, on the second level of the Jutila Center, was established in fall 2006. Art and design major Anna Sanchez was the gallery's first director. "My experience as director … has been invaluable and incredibly enlightening," she says in the summer 2007 *Bridge*. "I have learned the steps and processes involved in the work of a professional gallery director that can only be learned by actually taking on the job." (6)

Pictured: The opening reception for artist Terry Daulton in November 2008 (right), an exhibit of work by Kristin Stanchina in September 2012 (above), and a "Traveling Journal" exhibit in January 2011 (above right).

Mother and daughter Kathy Fisher (left, '07) and Samantha Fisher ('08) attended and played women's hockey at Finlandia.

C. J. Fisher ('08), son and brother, also attended and played hockey at the university.

In the winter 2006 *Bridge* Ubbelohde revisits his five "Ps" of marketing in a review of the previous 16 years. That *Bridge* issue also announced and illustrated a "Vision for Excellence" capital campaign focused on the improvement of plant and facilities.

"[In 1990] With limited financial resources, we focused our efforts on program *(product)* change and transformed ourselves into a four-year institution with academic and admission standards," Ubbelohde writes. "As part of our effort to communicate *(promotion)* these changes to prospective students, we changed our name to Finlandia University." (2)

With the final class of A.D.N. graduates, the nursing program's conversion to a four-year B.S.N. was complete in spring 2003—as was Finlandia's conversion to a four-year university—and strategic focus was shifted to the fifth "P," *people*. By 2006, 40% of faculty members had, or were pursuing, terminal academic degrees, and an effort began to increase salaries on par with other ELCA-affiliated colleges and universities. Similarly, *price* (tuition and fees) was positioned within the university's peer group of ELCA colleges and universities. Finally, strategic focus was concentrated on *place*, improving out-of-date facilities and in general working to make campus both more functional and attractive.

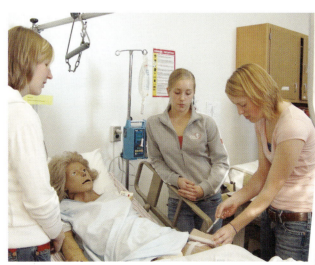

Nursing students in 2006-07.

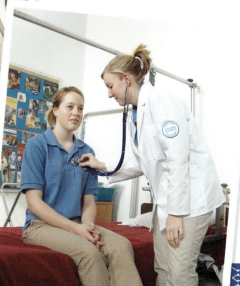

2006-07 Lion's Roar student newspaper staff (left to right): Tim Jaska, Lauren (Roell) Schwartz ('07), Steve Palek ('08), Brandon Gassi, and Ben LaComb ('09).

Associate professor of English Suzanne Van Dam (second from left) with students Maggie Seppala, Carmen Dunstan ('07), and Jessica Skop in 2006.

A group of high school-age basketball players from Tampere, Finland, visited campus June 19-21, 2006, as part of a 12-day cultural exchange trip organized by the Marquette (Michigan) Magic Amateur Athletic Union Basketball Club. The Finnish youth belong to Tampereen Pyrintö (TP), Tampere's largest sports club for youth 15 to 20 years old.

Art and design students created a series of paintings in 2006 that hangs in a hallway at Portage Health, Hancock. Pictured are (left to right): Mary Jones-Gundersen ('06), Carrice McKinstry ('08), Yu-Han Liaw ('07), and Ben Mitchell ('10).

2007

In January 2007 more than 100 students registered for the university's first online courses. In fall 2007 the Suomi College of Arts & Sciences added a concentration in Christian vocation and two B.A. in Liberal Studies majors: English and social sciences.

In early 2007 the B.S.N. program was granted accreditation for a period of five-years, the maximum initial accreditation duration granted by the Commission on Collegiate Nursing Education (CCNE). The program has been accredited continuously since.

More than 100 years of history arrived at the Finnish American Heritage Center in spring 2007. "A very large unit of Finnish-American history is now safely inside our climate-controlled archive," said Heritage Center director James Kurtti of the collection of Knights of Kaleva records—some from as early as the mid-1890s—donated by the organization's Grand Lodge, Virginia, Minnesota. (Summer 2007 *Bridge* 9)

The Class of 2007 included the first B.S.N. graduates.

What is it like to be a nurse in Finland?
What are nursing education and health care like there?

From April 26 to May 10, 2007, four Finlandia nursing sophomores learned first-hand the answers to these questions as part of a student and faculty exchange agreement between Finlandia and Helsinki Polytechnic Stadia. The study abroad opportunity, part of the three-credit course Finlandia Connection (NUR 301), was conducted for several years.

Pictured are 2008 Finlandia Connection course participants in Helsinki with nursing instructor Debbie Kartsu (far left) and President Johnson (third from left).

In March 2007 Philip Johnson was appointed Finlandia's 16th president, effective July 1, 2007. As the lead author and coordinator of the university's 2007 self-study accreditation report for the Higher Learning Commission, Johnson had become well-acquainted with the university.

In the summer 2007 *Bridge* Johnson reflects on three core competencies that will guide his university leadership. The first, missional integrity, "means our programs and activities are aligned with who we are and what we want to become," he explains. The second core competency is financial stability, an acute challenge for all small, private, enrollment-dependent liberal arts colleges. The third, meaningful community, is "doing community well … creating a deeper sense of shared purpose and vision, and enhancing collegiality. … [and exploration of] ever-fresh ways to be neighborly, to find shared solutions … with the city of Hancock and other Copper Country communities." (11)

"Knowing Philip Johnson, I know his commitment to the liberal arts and disciplined inquiry, his respect for the beliefs of those of other faiths, his understanding of our need to encourage global connections, and his sensitivity to the history and heritage of Finlandia and the university's relationship with the region we serve. … As Philip shares his vision for Finlandia, I have confidence that it will reflect and bring focus to the aspirations and hopes of the broad Finlandia community. … In Philip and René, [Susan and I] believe Finlandia has found good leadership." (2)

President Johnson with students in fall 2007.
Photo by Adam Johnson.

In spring 2007 twenty-two university students, faculty, and staff spent their spring break helping recover the hurricane-ravaged city of New Orleans. "We have so much and the people in New Orleans have so little left. Knowing that we brought hope to even one person made every hot, dirty, sticky, and tiring part of our work completely worth it," said elementary education junior Kari Noll ('09). (Summer 2007 *Bridge* 13)

On April 26, 2007, a three-panel mural depicting the history of the Copper Country, painted by a team of art and design students, was transported to the Carnegie Cultural Museum, Houghton, and installed in the museum's entryway. As the team's leader, studio arts senior Christine Sommerfeldt kept everyone on task. "It took a lot of communication and coordination to keep everyone on the same wave length," she said. (Summer 2007 *Bridge* 7-8).

Pictured with two panels of the mural are: (left to right) Melissa Gronoski, Kourtney Wojdyla, D. C. Wilson ('10), Benjamin Mitchell ('10), faculty member Yueh-mei Cheng, Courtney VanWagner, Allie Wurzer, Christine Sommerfeldt ('07), and Lana Bosak ('10).

Bob Ubbelohde waves good bye and he and Susan Ubbelohde admire a farewell gift they received May 17, 2007, at a dinner in their honor at the Paavo Nurmi Center.

Robert Ubbelohde retired June 30, 2007. "Under the leadership of Bob and Susan Ubbelohde during the past fifteen years Finlandia University has experienced unprecedented change and growth, all for the better," says Dale Skogman, chair of the university's board, in the spring 2007 *Bridge*. "During their tenure the core strengths of Finlandia have been enhanced and the Finnish, Lutheran, and liberal arts roots of the university have been reenergized."

For these reasons, and many more, the board endorsed a number of resolutions to recognize the Ubbelohdes' contributions to the growth of university. One of them is the Robert and Susan Ubbelohde Endowment for Religious Life, another was awarding to Ubbelohde the title of president emeritus.

When Ubbelohde is asked to identify his greatest accomplishments as president, he replies, "I don't even think that way. What I think about are students crossing the stage at Commencement … I can't claim to know the life story of each student, but … I know when a graduate has overcome or accomplished something extraordinary to earn that degree. To me, that's significant." (Spring 2007 *Bridge* 14-15)

"I tried to keep track of the small details for Robert," Susan Ubbelohde says in the spring 2007 *Bridge*. "It was important for him to concentrate on the big picture. I was comfortable with that."

President Ubbelohde congratulates a Class of 2007 graduate.

2007 Commencement, April 29.

"This place is so amazing. In one sense it's in the middle of nowhere and not very big, but on the other hand there are so many things happening," Susan says in the same article, citing the college's 100th anniversary celebration and the annual Sibelius Festival in particular. "If anyone had told me I was going to spend this much time in the Upper Peninsula, I would have told them they were crazy."(6-7)

"Any leadership, at least for someone who's married, is a joint thing," President Ubbelohde says in the spring 2007 *Bridge*. "Susan has been a tremendous help to me and my work, and an asset to the university … It goes beyond taking care of Board dinners, organizing the Sibelius Festival, and all that she's done for North Wind Books." (15)

"Robert and Susan Ubbelohde exemplify the ideal university president and first lady," remark Ray and Lois Lescelius in the spring 2007 *Bridge*, noting especially the Ubbelohdes' "friendly, generous and upbeat personalities" and their business and education expertise. (20) Ray Lescelius served on the university board from 2002 to 2007.

"Twenty-five years ago it was my impression that in order to survive Suomi College had to revive its mission," writes Esko Häkli, university trustee and retired director of the Helsinki University Library (which is the national library of Finland), in the spring 2006 *Bridge*. "It's amazing to see how the present Finlandia University … has grown. It has utilized its Finnish background to establish dynamic contacts with Finland and has developed these contacts into sources of new inspiration and new programs. Finlandia has become an institution with an international orientation." (5)

"Bob will be remembered for his perseverance, his stick-to-it-iveness. He didn't give up on anything," said emeritus board member Sandy (Alexander) McAfee. (Spring 2007 *Bridge* 22)

Left: The Finlandia University board of trustees in May 2007.

On May 19, 2007, historic action was taken to downsize the Finlandia University board. The result, as provided for in changes to Finlandia's constitution and by-laws, was a smaller, more effective governing body of 15-25 members, and a four-member executive committee. "In their foresight in advocating change, former president Robert Ubbelohde, former board chair Dale Skogman, along with members of the prior board, are to be commended for this bold action," says Sylvia Fleishman, board chair from 2007 to 2011, in the winter 2007 *Bridge*. (5)

Jessica Millar ('09) removes from the oven a batch of just-baked cookies at Finlandia Hall in December 2007.

Students participate in a statewide beach clean-up day at McLain State Park on September 23, 2007.

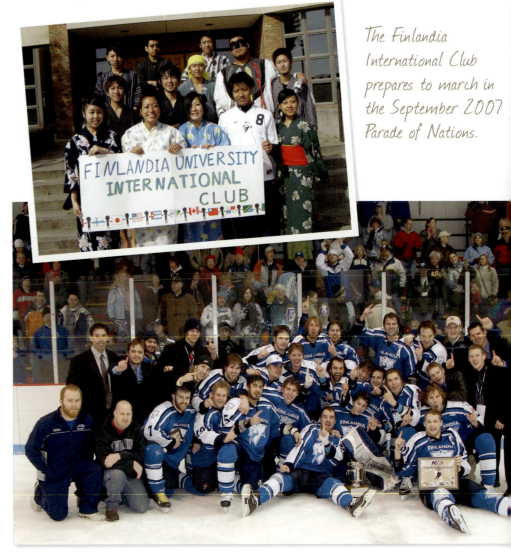

The Finlandia International Club prepares to march in the September 2007 Parade of Nations.

At a final four contest on March 11 hosted at the Houghton County Arena, Hancock, the Finlandia men's hockey team, coached by Joe Burcar, captured the 2007 Midwest Collegiate Hockey Association (MCHA) Harris Cup in a "dramatic come-from-behind 4-3 thriller" over two-time defending champion Milwaukee School of Engineering. Josh Paquette ('08), Ryan Sullivan ('09), and Marc (Tiger) Marcotte ('10) were named to the MCHA All-Conference Team. (Summer 2007 *Bridge* 17)

"On September 20 (2007), after days of dreary weather, the sun finally came out to help welcome into office the sixteenth president of Finlandia University, Rev. Dr. Philip R. Johnson," declares an article by students Pamela Kotila ('10) and Jessie Millar ('09) in the winter 2007 *Bridge*. "Anyone in the general vicinity of the Paavo Nurmi Center could not but be drawn towards the sound of the drumming and chanting of Four Thunders Drum. … Inside, the flags of many countries were hung from the ceiling, and the stage was adorned with potted birch trees, symbolizing our strong Finnish heritage." (12)

Above: President Johnson accepts the presidential regalia from board chair Sylvia Fleishman.

CHAPTER TEN

2008 to 2013: Shared Challenges, Shared Solutions

President Philip Johnson.

"If you want to hear stories of sisu, just talk to our students. There is no sisu shortage here," said President Johnson at his inauguration in September 2007. "This is why Finlandia, I like to say, matters. We are here to embolden and enable men and women of all ages and seasons in life to seek a college degree that perhaps was thought to be out of reach—and, once reached, inspires us all, certainly me … [Finlandia pursues] a courageous mission serving courageous students."

Since 2007 President Philip Johnson has advanced Finlandia's mission with new initiatives in planning, governance and finance reform, campus leadership, and visioning. Framing the university's current strategic plan is Campus and Community: Together for Good, a partnership which draws on and builds community relationships and targets enrollment growth through the College of Health Sciences and NCAA Division III athletics.

2008

In early 2008 James Kurtti, Finnish American Heritage Center director and editor of the *Finnish American Reporter*, was appointed Honorary Consul of Finland for the Upper Peninsula of Michigan; he succeeded Robert Ubbelohde.

Two B.F.A. concentrations were introduced in fall 2008: a cross-disciplinary major that incorporates two or more art and design disciplines, and an interdisciplinary design major (now the integrated design major) that merges learning in product, interior, and sustainable design. "There's value in not becoming too specialized," says associate professor of art and design Rick Loduha in the winter 2008 *Bridge*. "The interdisciplinary design degree addresses what we have to change to make a sustainable world. Mainstream design professions are finally beginning to recognize and embrace the absolute necessity of sustainable design." (11)

In fall 2008 B.F.A. graduates Fred Knoch ('09) and Ansley Knoch ('09) studied product design and garment design, respectively, at HAMK University of Applied Sciences, Hameenlinna, Finland. Here they are pictured at Suomenlinna, an island in Helsinki with an historic sea fortress. Photo by 2003 Sibelius Festival pianist Joonas Ahonen.

Ansley Knoch (left, '09) and Elyse Beebe ('11).

Jessica Spear ('11).

Art students participate in a book-binding workshop in the 2008 spring semester.

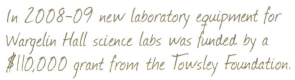

In 2008-09 new laboratory equipment for Wargelin Hall science labs was funded by a $110,000 grant from the Towsley Foundation.

The Sustainable Keweenaw Resource Center (SKRC) was established in 2008. Housed in the Jutila Center, the SKRC provides resources for creating sustainable communities in the Keweenaw Peninsula, including the Keweenaw Green Directory, a free online database of locally available green products and services.

The university's entrance sign, dedicated October 18, 2008, was coordinated by President Johnson and funded by the Finlandia University President's Council in recognition of Robert and Susan Ubbelohde's service to the university from 1988 to 2007. The sign was designed by Lang Yue of the Frank Lloyd Wright School of Architecture at Taliesin, in cooperation with the International School of Art & Design. Pictured, left to right, are Melissa Gronowski ('08), Sylvia Fleishman, Elsa Brule, Marvin Suomi, Susan Ubbelohde, Robert Ubbelohde, Bill Sauey, Paul Halme, and Ava Anttila.

Sibelius Academy Music Festival performers clarinetist Kaisa Koivula (left) and accordionist Jukka Ojala at the Vertin Gallery, Calumet, in August 2008.

Elementary education majors in fall 2008 (left to right): Jamie Bellinger ('10), Mike Datto ('09), Serena Harju ('10), Lisa Harden ('09), Gina Aho ('09), Alisha Carne ('09), and Heidi Butler ('09).

2008-09 Student Senate members Jillian Dolkey ('10), Justin Buzzo ('10), and Ally Tincknell ('10).

In the 2007-08 men's basketball season Tyler Gordon ('11) amassed 99 steals in 25 games—an average of 4.0 per game and an NCAA-wide record.

Annually each December since 1917 Finlandia University has observed Finland's Independence Day with a public program of Finnish music and culture. Pictured are Finnish nationals at the 2010 Finland Independence Day program performing a scene from "Tiernapojat" (Star Boys), a traditional Finnish Christmas play. Pictured at the 2008 observance are kantele players Kay Seppala, Bette Premo, Dave Bezotte, and René Johnson.

The Finlandia Pep Band in spring 2008.

The Sanders' Club, a group of volunteers coordinated by Don Peryam ('68), hosted a pie social in December 2008 to raise funds for replacement of the lower level windows of Old Main, one of many campus improvement projects undertaken by the group in the 2000s and early 2010s. Pictured are (left to right): Norma Nominelli, Nancy Fenton, Hazel Tepsa, Charleen Ahola, Lois Seaton, and Don Peryam.

Pekka Lintu, ambassador of Finland to the U.S., presented the commencement address April 27, 2008. Lintu concluded his speech with the Finnish proverb, "Minkä ilotta oppii, sen surutta unohtaa" or "What you learn without joy, you will forget without sorrow."

Steve Palek ('08) accepts from Rev. Carolyn Raffensperger a 2008 Good News Award for his article, "A Look at an Unusual Mind," published in the November 23, 2007, issue of the Finlandia University student newspaper, *The Roar*. The Good News Awards—sponsored by the Presbyterian, United Methodist, Catholic, Episcopal, and Evangelical Lutheran churches in the Upper Peninsula region—honor radio, television, and newspaper productions that touch hearts and minds.

Class of 2008 graduates Kathryn Holsworth and Travis Hanson.

Commencement, April 27, 2008.

2009

In January 2009 Finlandia was awarded a dual Community Engagement Classification, for Curricular Engagement and Outreach and Partnerships, from The Carnegie Foundation for the Advancement of Teaching. The classification recognizes excellent alignment of the university's mission, culture, leadership, resources, and practices in support of dynamic and noteworthy community engagement.

In early 2009 Finlandia University, Hancock Public Schools, and the city of Hancock launched Campus and Community: Together for Good, a strategic, creative exchange of physical school district properties for a long-term package of Finlandia tuition awards and educational programs and services.

"Hancock and Finlandia face many common challenges for growth in a context where resources are not in abundance," says Johnson in the spring 2009 *Bridge*. "These shared challenges invite, even urge, shared solutions." (12)

Over the life of the 12-year agreement, the swap will net $4.2 million in scholarships for Hancock Central High School graduates who attend Finlandia (the Hancock Award), and the university gained ownership of two Hancock Public Schools properties: a 73,000 square foot historic middle school building on Quincy Street and the 11.4-acre Condon Field on Birch Street. A joint committee of representatives from Hancock Public Schools, the city of Hancock, and Finlandia University oversees the agreement.

Above: A reunion of 1950s and 1960s alumni, with special recognition of Suomi Seminary graduates, was hosted in June 2008.

Campus and Community: Together for Good garnered national media coverage, including an article and photo on page four of the July 10, 2009, issue of the *Chronicle of Higher Education*, a national Associate Press article carried by hundreds of U.S. newspapers and other media outlets (including CNN News on September 8 and *USA Today* on September 15), and Johnson's September 17, 2009, appearance on FOXBusiness.com LIVE. Pictured are Johnson (right) and John Sanregret, principal of Hancock Central High School. Photo by Michael Kienitz for the Associated Press.

Finlandia Hall move-in day, August 19, 2009.

Fifty-eight Hancock Central High School graduates, recipients of Finlandia's Hancock Award, are pursing degrees at Finlandia as of spring 2013. Pictured are nine of the fall 2009 Hancock Award freshmen on the steps of Old Main. As of spring 2013, five Hancock Award recipients have completed bachelor's degrees at Finlandia and six have completed associate degrees.

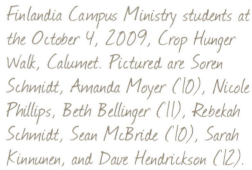

Finlandia Campus Ministry students at the October 4, 2009, Crop Hunger Walk, Calumet. Pictured are Soren Schmidt, Amanda Moyer ('10), Nicole Phillips, Beth Bellinger ('11), Rebekah Schmidt, Sean McBride ('10), Sarah Kinnunen, and Dave Hendrickson ('12).

In fall 2009 the Finlandia men's soccer program became an affiliate member of the Wisconsin Intercollegiate Athletic Conference (WIAC). Pictured is a September 2011 soccer game at Finlandia's McAfee Field. Photos by Leah Kanost.

"I see it as a very positive thing for the entire community," said Hancock Mayor Bill Laitala of the Campus and Community partnership. "That the growth of Finlandia's health care programs is part of the focus is very good for community, and right on track for national health care worker needs. It should also be good for recruiting students. For the city of Hancock, the better Finlandia does, the better the community does. I hope the plan will be a great success." (Spring 2009 *Bridge* 12)

"Officials from the Hancock Public Schools and Finlandia University should be congratulated for thinking outside the box and coming up with creative solutions for difficult situations … the synergy of these two proud educational institutions working together can only lead to more positives within each school," states an editorial in the January 22, 2009, *Daily Mining Gazette* of Houghton, Michigan.

Fall 2009 enrollment, at 568 students, increased nine percent over fall 2008 enrollment and included 259 incoming freshmen, readmitted students, and transfer students, and 309 returning students.

Finlandia students have published a newspaper, *The Roar*, since the early 2000s. Pictured is the 2008-09 Student Senate with a printing press purchased that academic year. They are (left to right): Michaela Boddy ('11), Ally Tincknell ('11), Justin Buzzo ('11), Jillian Dolkey ('10), Liz Reno ('09), and Jessie Millar ('09). As *The Roar* is now completely online, the press is no longer in use.

Students chop wood for Little Brothers Friends of the Elderly in winter 2009. University chaplain Soren Schmidt is pictured in the foreground.

The Certificate of Occupancy permit for the renovated sixth and seventh floors of the Jutila Center was signed December 29—exactly four years after the EDA contract was signed in 2005. The two new floors added 20 incubator suites, for a total of 42. In spring 2013, 32 businesses were leasing Jutila Center suites, providing 47 jobs. Pictured at the December 18, 2009, dedication are (left to right): Finlandia trustee Ken Seaton, Jutila Center director Bonnie Holland, and President Johnson. Seaton is being presented with a gift as the dedication happened to fall on his 80th birthday.

January 2009 Homecoming Obstacle Course Race champions (left to right): back row: Dale Rogers, Jordan Siegler ('09), Sami Horst ('10), Jessie Millar ('09), Stephanie Trevino ('11); front: Amanda Moyer ('11) and Kumiko Takahashi ('09).

Class of 2009 graduate Salome Mnzava, an international student from Tanzania.

In November 2009 members of the Finlandia men's and women's basketball team helped assemble 24,000 meals for a Thrivent Financial fundraiser in Tacoma, Washington, to benefit orphaned children in Africa and South America. The student-athletes were in Washington to participate in a tournament hosted by Pacific Lutheran University. Pictured are (left to right): front row: Casey Luke ('09), Amy Bellinger ('10), Deanna Makela ('11), Sasha Beyers, Jeannette Katona ('09), Lindsey Antilla ('09); back: Kaitlin Voigt ('11), Dawn Engman ('12), Jillian Dolkey ('10), Jodi Riutta ('12), Ally Tincknell ('11), Linzy Monticello ('09), Coach Curtis Wittenberg, and Jamie Bellinger ('10).

A three-panel, 12-foot by 5-foot oil painting by Finnish artist Aarno Karimo, donated to Suomi College in 1946 by Finland's Suomi-Seura (Finland Society), was hung in the Finnish American Heritage Center in fall 2009. The painting, which hung in Nikander Hall's White Pine Room for many years, had been in storage. The painting commemorates the 300th anniversary of the Delaware (Maryland) Settlement and honors that community's Finnish immigrants; its frame is constructed of wood salvaged from a church in Karelia built around the same time as the founding of the settlement. The mural is pictured behind kantele players at the December 1, 2011, Finland Independence Day observance.

"Keweenaw Wildflowers Up Close," an exhibit of wildflower photography by Harvey Desnick, is on permanent display on the sixth floor of Finlandia's Jutila Center campus.

In direct response to the priority personnel needs of local and regional health care providers, in fall 2009 the College of Health Sciences established a five-semester certified medical assistant (CMA) associate degree program. In fall 2012 the program was accredited for a period of five years by the Commission on Accreditation of Allied Health Education Programs. Like the CMA program, each of Finlandia's College of Health Sciences programs have earned and sustained continuous independent accreditation by their respective accrediting organizations.

Finlandia's CMA degree is the Upper Peninsula's only accredited medical assistant program. A 2010 grant from Thrivent Financial helped jump start the CMA program, providing funds to equip and furnish a state-of-the art classroom and lab. Diplomas were awarded to the first class of medical assistant graduates in spring 2011.

Also in fall 2009, the Suomi College of Arts & Sciences added B.A. in Liberal Studies majors in psychology, communication, and criminal justice, and the human services bachelor degree program began a transition to an associate of arts degree program.

A Campus Read was introduced in fall 2009. Selections to date are *The Gendarme* by Mark Mustian in 2013, and *Into the Wild* by Jon Krakauer in 2012.

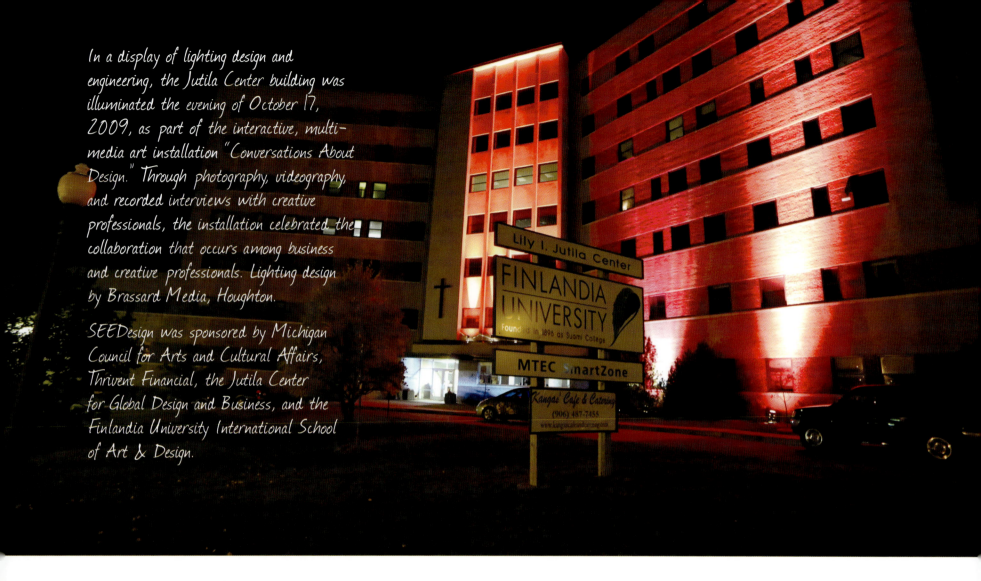

In a display of lighting design and engineering, the Jutila Center building was illuminated the evening of October 17, 2009, as part of the interactive, multi-media art installation "Conversations About Design." Through photography, videography, and recorded interviews with creative professionals, the installation celebrated the collaboration that occurs among business and creative professionals. Lighting design by Brassard Media, Houghton.

SEEDesign was sponsored by Michigan Council for Arts and Cultural Affairs, Thrivent Financial, the Jutila Center for Global Design and Business, and the Finlandia University International School of Art & Design.

Phase Two renovations to the Jutila Center, begun in January 2009, were completed in November 2009. Improvements included replacement of the roof, replacement of the windows on floors five to nine, upgrades to the plumbing, electrical, and fire suppression systems, a second boiler, a second elevator, and renovation of floors six and seven. The work continued a multi-phase project funded by a $952,800 EDA matching grant awarded in 2005. Overall through 2009, $4.7 million has been invested in renovations to the Jutila Center, which houses Finlandia's International School of Art & Design; the university's small business incubator, the Center for Global Design and Business; and the MTEC SmartZone technology business incubator.

"The Western Upper Peninsula Planning and Development Region (WUPPDR) helped us facilitate both phases of the public/private project, and we've also worked closely with UP Engineers and Architects and other local partners to make this happen," says Jutila Center director Bonnie Holland in the summer/fall 2009 *Bridge*. "Community support was essential to progress this far with Jutila Center renovations." (22)

2010

In April 2010 President Johnson and Gogebic Community College (GCC) president Jim Lorenson signed a Memorandum of Understanding and Articulation Agreement. The agreement's course equivalency sheets clearly delineate how a GCC student can minimize duplication of academic requirements and smoothly transition from completion of a two-year GCC degree program to a degree program at Finlandia.

Fall 2010 student enrollment, at 673, was the largest fall enrollment in 25 years, the highest since four-year degrees were introduced in 1996, and an 18% increase over the previous fall. "This year's enrollment growth is extraordinary," says Johnson in the fall/winter 2010 *Bridge*. "We have met or exceeded three key strategic goals in retention, recruitment, and resident student numbers. This is exactly what Finlandia needs." (8)

In fall 2010 the International School of Business (ISB) reintroduced its 2+2 B.B.A. in applied management, which is tailored for students who have completed an associate degree, and introduced a B.B.A. major in arts management.

Per the Campus and Community: Together for Good initiative, ownership of the former Hancock Middle School and Condon Athletic Field was officially transferred to Finlandia March 26, 2010. Johnson is pictured with Monica Healy, superintendent of Hancock Public Schools.

Finlandia cheerleaders march in the January 2010 Heikinpäivä parade in downtown Hancock. Pictured are (left to right): Sara Spangler ('13), Rebecca Ward ('14), and Cayla Raymaker ('11).

Alex Malasusa, bishop of the Evangelical Lutheran Church in Tanzania (ELCT) Eastern and Coastal Diocese, presented the May 2, 2010, commencement address and received an honorary doctorate.

Class of 2011 valedictorian Meisha Bray receives her B.S.N. pin from Fredi deYampert, nursing department chair and professor, on May 2, 2011.

Pictured are women's hockey team members at the January 2010 downtown Hancock Heikinpäivä Parade. They are (left to right): Jackie D'Urso, Kelly Poelstra ('12, '13), Chelsea Pollard, and Nicole Schumacher ('12).

Once or twice annually for several decades, university play productions were directed by faculty members Melvin Kangas and Dan Maki, with players including Finlandia students, faculty and staff, and community members.

March 2008: "Two by Two." Pictured at the far right is Dan Maki, play director.

October 2008: "Mr. Puntila and His Man Matti" (Herr Puntila und sein Knecht Matti) by Bertolt Brecht. Pictured seated (above right) are Pasi Lautala and Kendra Benson ('13); standing (above) are Hannu Leppanen and Phyllis Fredendall; directed by Melvin Kangas.

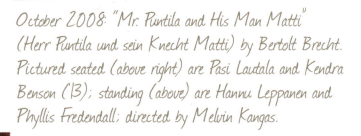

November 2007: "At the Hawk's Well," an experimental Japanese "Noh" drama by W. B. Yeats. Pictured is Oren Tikkanen; directed by Melvin Kangas.

October 2009: "Women of Niskavuori" (Niskavuoren naiset) by Hella Wuolijoki. Pictured are (left to right): Kaisa Randolph, Ren Olsen, Pam Puotto, MacKenzie Murtamaki, and Kristen Tepsa; directed and translated from the Finnish and adapted for the American stage by Melvin Kangas. "Women of Niskavuori" is one of a series of popular plays Wuolijoki wrote between 1936 and 1953 about the people who live and work at a large manorial farm, Niskavuori, in the western Finland province of Häme. Kangas translated and directed three installments of the drama.

October 2011: "On Approval" by Frederick Lonsdale. Pictured are Sunny K. (left) and Soren Schmidt; directed by Melvin Kangas.

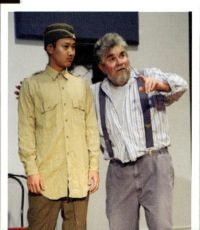

November 2012: "What Now, Niskavuori," by Hella Wuolijoki Pictured at far left are (left to right): Diane Miller, René Johnson, and Pam Puotto. Standing are 2013 graduate Tomoyuki Ishizuka (left) and Dan Maki.

A Pep Band concert December 2, 2010. Pictured are (left to right): Sarah Schumacher, Chisato Ota ('12), and Rei Hirakawa ('11).

A University Singers concert, April 22, 2010.

Class of 2010 nursing graduates Christina Andres (left) and Roxanne McCabe.

The university's Alumni Board and the Office of Alumni Relations hosted a three-day all-class reunion June 25 to June 27, 2010. Pictured are members of the Class of 1960 (left to right): front row: Alice (Heikkila) Kinnunen, Lorna (Niemi) O'Reilly; middle: Beth (Mattson) Glasoe, Jeanne (Wierimaa) Kemppainen, Judy (Bowlus) Bye, Marilynn (Johnson) Baldwin, Karen (Malila) Palmer, Joy (Kesatie) Lake, Marsha (Galazen) Mellen; back: Paul Nomellini, John O'Reilly.

Art and design student Dominic Fredianelli (right) painted this 12-foot by 100-foot mural on the south-facing exterior wall of Finlandia's Jutila Center campus in fall 2011. The mural depicts Fredianelli's National Guard deployments to Iraq. Fredianelli is one of several Copper Country National Guard soldiers whose stories are told in the Emmy Award-winning 2011 documentary film "Where Soldiers Come From."

Two annual spring semester exhibitions at the Finlandia University Gallery feature the artwork of International School of Art & Design (ISAD) students. Student-submitted artwork exhibited in the Juried Student Exhibition is selected by a jury composed of a faculty member, a graduating ISAD senior, and a community member. The ISAD Diploma Works exhibit showcases the work of graduating B.F.A. seniors.

Left: The B.F.A. Class of 2010 at the 2010 Diploma Works exhibit.

Below: Diploma Works Exhibit artwork, April 2011.

"But By This Path," book illustrations by Josh Jaehnig.

"Desire Path," by Audrey Chamberlain.

Jewelry by Elyse Beebe.

Clothing design by Rachel Reidenga.

Juried Student Exhibit artwork, March 2012.

Abigail Knight.

Below: "Before the Man on the Moon," by Ashley Hoeper.

Front: "Guardian of Wisdom," by Ashlee Kranz.
Back: "Fallen," by Sascha Hirzel.

"Being Different," book illustrations by Margo Anderson.

2011

The university announced in spring 2011 that its elementary education B.A. in liberal studies would no longer accept new students. Junior and senior elementary education majors in good standing were able to complete their Finlandia degrees and eligibility to apply for Michigan teaching licensure was not affected. "This was a difficult decision but, ultimately, we are certain that it is in the best interest of both our students and the university," says Johnson in the spring 2001 *Bridge*. (10)

In June 2011 President Johnson, TyAnn Lindell, Finlandia EVP for academic affairs, and Bay College president Laura Coleman signed a Memorandum of Understanding and Articulation Agreement. The agreement's equivalency sheets clearly delineate how a Bay College student can minimize duplication of academic requirements and smoothly transition from completion of a two-year Bay College degree program to a degree program at Finlandia.

In fall 2011 the Suomi College of Arts & Sciences introduced bachelor of arts in liberal studies programs in sociology and pre-professional science, and added minors in business administration, fine art, and graphic design.

In fall 2011 The International School of Business (ISB) announced an agreement with Jeffers High School, Painesdale, Michigan, and the Copper Country Intermediate School District in which Jeffers High School juniors and seniors who complete with a final grade of "A" the courses Business, Management and Administration I and/or II qualify to receive tuition-free college credit for Finlandia courses Fundamentals of Business (BUS 138) and Introductory Computer Applications (CIS 102). Terry Monson, dean of Finlandia's Business School, explains that Jeffers graduates who enroll at Finlandia and take advantage of the agreement will get a head start on a bachelor of business administration (BBA) or other Finlandia University degree.

Homecoming, January 2011.

The university's elementary education program participated with the Community Coalition on Grief and Bereavement in an annual spring semester "Art from the Grieving Heart" writing competition from 2007 to 2012, when the contest was discontinued. Students and faculty participated in judging entries and prepared lesson plans on coping with grief for use by school teachers in the counties of Baraga, Houghton, Keweenaw, and Ontonagon.

Above: Lisa Oysti congratulates a 2011 writing competition awardee.

The Young Women's Caucus for Art, an internal caucus of the Women's Caucus for Art (WCA), was established by Finlandia students in 2009. Here, International School of Art & Design students and alumnae gather in New York City for the WAC's annual conference in spring 2011.

Pictured are J. R. Demers ('11), Dawn Hilts ('13), Jaimianne Amicucci ('10), New York artist Bonnie McAllister, Amanda Mears ('12), Amanda Moyer ('11), Stephanie Trevino ('11), and Susie Danielson ('11).

In January 2011 the Finnish American Historical Archive received a significant artifacts donation from Ethel Suominen of Brooklyn, New York, in memory of her late husband, Veikko Suominen. The majority of the objects are from Mr. Suominen's Finland birthplace, the Suominen farm in the former parish of Rymättylä (now Naantali) of southwest Finland. The 100-piece collection includes 19th century household and farm objects, ice skates, home-made fishing nets, equestrian equipment, ice walkers, and numerous other hand-made 19th century household items and tools.

Completion of the $2.3 million, phase one construction of the Finlandia University Athletic Complex was celebrated August 31, 2011, at a tailgating event at McAfee Field. The all-weather competition surface, stadium lighting, and electronic scoreboard were formally dedicated September 23, 2011, during halftime of a football game between the Hancock Central High School Bulldogs and the Calumet High School Copper Kings. The new athletic field is home turf for Finlandia men's and women's soccer and the Hancock Central High School football team, and supports other community sports associations and recreational activities. McAfee Field was designated the 2011 Keweenaw Chamber of Commerce Project of the Year.

Groundbreaking for McAfee Field, named for board trustee and major donor Alexander (Sandy) McAfee, took place May 20, 2011.

Students pictured are (left to right): Nick Hendrickson ('14), Riku F. Lion, Dawn Engman ('12), and Haley Laban ('11).

Pictured are (left to right): Riku F. Lion, Hancock mayor Bill Laitala, Sandy McAfee, athletic director Chris Salani, Hancock Central High School principal John Sanregret, trustee John Stierna, and President Johnson.

The men's soccer team trains at McAfee Field in fall 2011.

Cameron Goude (right, '13) and Nemanja Jankovic ('12) at McAfee Field.

Above: Athletic director Chris Salani, EVP for external relations Duane Aho, and President Johnson at McAfee Field in August 2011.

Left: President Johnson, Dennis Harbour, superintendent of the Copper Country Intermediate School District, and John Vaara, retired superintendent of Hancock Public Schools, on August 31, 2011, at the tailgating party.

The Ryan Street Community Garden, a university outreach activity on Ryan Street across from North Wind Books, marked its first growing season in spring 2011. The garden's 15 raised plots are rented and tended by Hancock community members and volunteers.

Bi-annually since 2009 the Suomi College of Arts & Sciences has hosted a series of spring semester author lectures in conjunction with ENG 203. Pictured are students enrolled in the spring 2011 course (left to right): Brittany Cummings ('13), Cody Mills, Emmett Heine ('12), Ashley Baker, and Jake Hubbard ('11).

The university's Finnish Council hosted its first annual Finnish Folk Music Camp July 12 to July 14, 2011, at Camp Lahti on Lake Superior's Rabbit Bay. More than 70 people of all ages and skill levels participated in kantele, fiddle, mandolin, and bones classes, and workshops to learn wood carving, birch bark weaving, and Finnish cooking, among other activities.

In November 2011 Art History III students and faculty took a three-day trip to Chicago to experience art first-hand. Other stops included the Kohler (Wisconsin) Design Center and the Milwaukee Art Museum. The field trip has been arranged annually since 1997.

Pictured is the 2011 group in Chicago, in the front are Jessica Ingold (left) and Cait Spera.

Since 2004, 25 Finlandia fiber and fashion design students have received annual merit-based grants from the New York-based Barbara L. Kuhlman Foundation—several of them more than once.

Pictured are the 2010-11 grantees (left to right): back row: Eric Hinsch ('13), Abbi Zablocki ('11), Eileen Sundquist ('12), Audrey Chamberlain, Sara Heikkinen, fiber arts professor Phyllis Fredendall; front: Amanda Moyer ('11) and Susie Danielson ('11).

The university dining hall was relocated from Mannerheim Hall to Finlandia Hall in fall 2011. The new 4,600 square foot multi-level cafeteria, constructed in summer 2011, includes raised seating, specialty food stations, enlarged kitchen areas, and new restrooms.

Pictured in October 2012 are international students (left to right): Chisato Ota (12), Jing Jiang (13), Li "Mimi" Lin, Tomoyuki Ishizuka (13), and Yusuke Okazaki.

A new 25-foot flagpole in front of the Finnish American Heritage Center was dedicated in December 2011. The flagpole and flag were funded by the Finlandia Alumni Board. On Sami Day, February 6, 2013, the Sami flag was flown.

The opening reception for the 20th annual Contemporary Finnish American Artist Series, a retrospective exhibit, was held December 1, 2011, in conjunction with the annual Finland Independence Day celebration. A 48-page soft-cover book published for the exhibition includes artist information and 19 full-color reproductions of the artwork featured in the exhibit. Pictured standing are (left to right): James Kurtti, Anneli Halonen, artist Bruce Niemi, Mrs. John Lundeen, artist Kathleen Oettinger, Hazel Tepsa, and Jim Junttonen. At the podium is Anneli Halonen, cultural counselor of the Embassy of Finland, Washington D.C. Finnish baked goods are often served following the Finland Independence Day program.

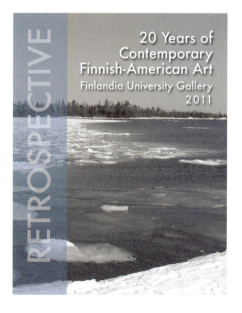

2012

In summer 2012 B.S.N. program accreditation was renewed for a period of ten years, the maximum accreditation duration awarded by the Commission on Collegiate Nursing Education (CCNE).

In fall 2012 Finlandia Athletics launched a junior varsity men's hockey program. The College of Arts & Sciences began a B.A. in Liberal Studies in art therapy, which was developed jointly by the schools of business and art and design. The International School of Business introduced a B.B.A. and a 2+2 B.B.A in healthcare management for students wishing to pursue management or administrative careers in the healthcare industry.

In spring 2012 the student-run FUEL Studio, a cross-curricular business and art and design initiative, was opened in the Jutila Center. The retail store sells art and other items created by students, faculty, alumni, and community members. Business major Scott Kalinec works the counter in April 2012.

Medical assistant students in January 2012 (left to right): back row: Robin Wakeham, Samantha Buth, Lauren Hodges, Sara McCue; center: Kelly Ylitalo, Jean Tracey, Heather Broniec, Tia Heikkinen; front: Jamie Clishe and Shelby Stevens. Each of these students graduated in spring 2012.

Paivi Hakkarainen, senior lecturer in media education at the University of Lapland, was a 2011-12 Fulbright Scholar-in-Residence at Finlandia. She taught two classes and in spring 2012 coordinated the pilot Hei Suomi! program, a collaborative annual project that engages South Range Elementary School third graders in learning about contemporary Finnish culture and language.

In spring 2012 the wide lawn in front of Finlandia's future College of Health Sciences building—variously referred to as "adjacent to the Heritage Center" or "in front of the historic middle school building"—was named the "Finlandia University Quincy Green."

In March 2012 Sanna-Mari Suopajärvi and Eeva Holappa, Finnish education students from the University of Lapland, explored with third graders at South Range (Michigan) Elementary School Finland's culture, geography, history, and traditions, as well as the everyday lives of Finnish children. The student-teachers employed educational technologies and teaching methods to engage students as active participants and explorers through an online blog and production of videos.

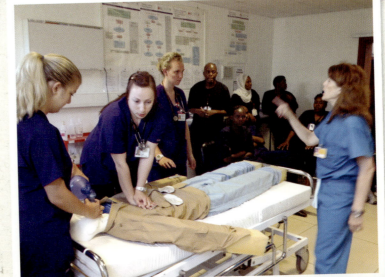

Finlandia nursing students conduct a cardiac resuscitation lesson at Muhimbili National Hospital in May 2012.

The Finlandia Student Nurses Organization was named a community service leader by the Michigan Student Nursing Association in spring 2012. The student-nurses were commended for their eighth annual spaghetti dinner and raffle in support of the Omega House hospice, Houghton. Since 2004 the student-nurses have donated to the Omega House more than $10,000 in dinner and raffle proceeds. Pictured are students at the seventh annual dinner February 26, 2011, at Gloria Dei Lutheran Church, Hancock.

At the dessert table is Amanda Constable who completed a B.A. in liberal studies in spring 2013. At the buffet table are Class of 2012 B.S.N. graduates Krystal (Luoma) Tormala (left) and Stephanie (Murray) Zychowski.

In a new healthcare component of the annual Service and Learning in Tanzania course, in May 2012 four Finlandia nursing students spent a week working side-by-side with Tanzanian student-nurses, nurses, and physicians at Muhimbili National Hospital in Dar es Salaam, the capital city of Tanzania.

Pictured on the hospital grounds are (left to right): Heidi Wingerson ('12), Ann Clancy-Klemme, Amanda Constable, and Lauren Belland. The healthcare component was developed by Mark Miron, assistant professor of nursing.

Summer 2012 campus improvement projects included the construction of new steps at the lower entrance to the Paavo Nurmi Center and installation of a new roof on Finlandia Hall.

An entry gate for the Ryan Street Community Garden, designed by Finlandia art and design student David Sarazin ('13), was installed in fall 2012. Funded by a mini-grant from the Michigan Council for the Arts and Cultural Affairs, the archway is constructed entirely of repurposed components. Pictured are David Sarazin (left) and Rick Loduha, associate professor of integrated design.

BikeFinlandia, a student-run pro-bike group, is working to build a fleet of low-cost rental bicycles for use on campus and in the community. Pictured in summer 2012 with bikes donated by the Hancock Police Department are students involved in the undertaking and faculty advisor Diane Miller (far left), assistant professor of communication.

Finlandia University's Student Senate

Below: The 2012-13 Student Senate. Each academic year the officers of the Student Senate are elected by student popular vote.

Riku and students cheer on the men's and women's soccer teams at McAfee Field in September 2012. Photo by Leah Kanost.

The 14th annual Finlandia University Sibelius Academy Music Festival, September 23 to September 28, 2012, included a "Meet the Musicians" event at the Finnish American Heritage Center. Pictured, seated, are pianist Pauli Jämsä (left) and cellist Liina Leijala. Performing is the contemporary folk music band "Hohka" with Meriheini Luoto (violin), Valtteri Lehto (kantele), Veikko Muikku (accordion) and Maksim Purovaara (bass).

Annually for several years, the Physical Therapist Assistant (PTA) Club has supported "Shoes 4 Kids," a national organization that provides shoes to children in need. Pictured are PTA students at the October 27, 2012, Soup for Sneakers lunch and silent auction fundraiser at the Finnish American Heritage Center.

Pictured are (left to right): PTA instructor Geri Hawley, Lars Pennala ('13), Amy Oja ('13), Alice Veley, Emily Turcotte, Jonica Rucinski ('13), Lori Stachowicz ('13), Emily Ragan ('13), Stacey Gray ('13), and Jason Gray.

2013

Current and recent Finlandia student clubs and organizations include Art and Painting Club, BikeFinlandia, Black Student Union (BSU), Bureau of Visible Thought (a writers' group), Campus Ministry, Curling Club, D'orcs of the North (games club), Entrepreneurship Club (CEO), Fiber Society, Finlandia Singers, FUEL Studio, International Club, intramural sports, Outdoor Club, Pep Band, Finlandia Pride Alliance, PTA Club, Reflection Gallery, *The Roar* student newspaper, Student Alumni Association, Student Athletic Advisory Committee, Student Nurses Organization, Student Senate, Student leaders, University Singers, and the Young Women's Caucus for Art.

Nicholas Stevens, EVP for finance, reports sustained improvement of the university's financial ratio in the winter 2009 *Bridge*, which he explains is an indicator of overall improvement in the institution's financial picture. (6) In 2013, Stevens shared more positive news: over the four-year period from June 30, 2008, to June 30, 2012, the university's net assets increased nearly 90%, from $16.7 million to $89.9 million; in the same period more than $10.4 million was invested in property, plant, and equipment.

Class of 2013 PTA students (left to right): Jennifer Britt, Deseray Pohjola, Melissa Wascher, and Jestina Poissant.

The 2012-13 men's golf team.

In fall 2013 Finlandia was authorized by the Higher Learning Commission to grant bachelor of arts degrees in specific disciplines of the arts and sciences, rather than the B.A. in Liberal Studies—approved by the HLC in the 1990s—with a concentration in a field of study. Thus, the current B.A. degree programs offered by the Suomi College of Arts & Sciences are in criminal justice, communication, English, pre-professional science, psychology, sociology, and social sciences.

The 2012-13 Finlandia Curling Club, coached by university chaplain Soren Schmidt, rose to the top of this national college club sport, earning a national ranking of #7 and competing against the top 16 college curling teams at the sport's national tournament in Duluth, Minnesota, in March 2013. At the tournament, the Finlandia curlers beat the College of St. Benedict/St. John's University—the #1 ranked team in the nation—9 to 7, and also showed well against Colgate University of New York and the University of Oklahoma, a state school with more than 20,000 undergraduates.

Finlandia's Office of the President coordinated two key events for FinnFest USA 2013, which was hosted by the university and the Copper Country community June 19 to June 23. The FinnFest USA 2013 Education Forum featured leading voices in Finnish education reform, including educator, teacher, and scholar Dr. Pasi Sahlberg. A service of celebration for the 50-year ministry of the Suomi Conference was led by ELCA presiding bishop Rev. Mark Hanson, with special guests from the Evangelical Lutheran Church of Finland.

Pictured above is the FinnFest USA 2013 board of directors (left to right): back row: Robin Bonini, Duane Aho, Scott MacInnes, Pete Negro, Dallas Bond, and Glenn Anderson; front: John Kiltinen, Pauline Kiltinen, Mary Pekkala, Hilary Virtanen, James Kurtti, David Maki, and Kevin Manninen.

Below: A Campus Read/Author Series 2013 discussion panel on April 2, 2013, in the Chapel of St. Matthew.

A women's softball scrimmage on September 30, 2012. Left: Alexis Lawley. Right: Alyson Herman (pitching) and Brierra Ruska (with mitt). Photos by Leah Kanost.

Athletic director Chris Salani congratulates the women's softball team April 24, 2013, on a great season as they start their journey to the 2013 Great South Athletic Conference tournament.

The 2012-13 women's softball team, coached by Shawn Hendrickson, finished the regular season with an overall win/loss record of 25-6, and won the Great South Athletic Conference (GSAC) softball championship April 27 with a 5-0 win over Huntington College. The GSAC championship earned the Lions an invitation to the NCAA Division III softball tournament, Finlandia's first NCAA tournament invitation in any sport.

A new entryway installed at the Finnish American Heritage Center in January 2011 (right) was the first of many recent improvements to the building. Other updates include installation of a climate-controlled display case in the archive's reading room, a fresh coat of paint for most FAHC areas, the addition of a kitchen area behind the theatre, and most recently the laying of a hardwood floor in the FAHC theatre. Additional upgrades were announced and dedicated at FinnFest USA in June 2013.

Left: A view of the theatre at the April 27, 2013, Diploma Works Exhibit reception.

Below: A contractor putting the finishing touches on the new wood floor.

Archivist Joanna Chopp with the custom-built display case in the Finnish American Historical Archive reading room.

CHAPTER ELEVEN

2014 to 2021: Envisioning Our Future

Commencement, April 28, 2013.

In a season of planning that began in October 2010, President Johnson, the board of trustees, and academic leadership began visioning and strategic thinking activities in preparation for the writing of a new strategic planning document for the years 2014 to 2021, when Finlandia University will celebrate its 125th anniversary.

Johnson values the long history and rich heritage that Suomi College, and now Finlandia University, proudly claim. "As we plan for Finlandia's 125th birthday, we will need to draw upon the courage and imagination of those who loved and led Finlandia through those earliest decades and beyond," he says. "I believe that our first thoughts must be of gratitude and praise for all those who have gone before and served so unselfishly—often in the midst of great adversity—her educational mission."

Building on his conviction that Finlandia's best self is already present within the university community, in spring 2012 Johnson began conducting the first of dozens of campus-wide visioning sessions to generate grass roots ideas for development of this new strategic plan.

President Philip Johnson.

Kristin DeJong, B.A.

Cameron Goude, B.A.

In small groups, faculty, staff, students, and community members reflected on Finlandia's best self, sharing ideas and convictions prompted by questions including: What does Finlandia look like at her best? What is the Finlandia experience? What is the fundamental purpose of undergraduate education? How do you define learning? When, where, and how does learning happen at Finlandia? What type of student thrives at Finlandia? What should a Finlandia degree mean? What kind of world awaits our graduates?

In spring 2013 the campus community again was invited to participate in collective reflection, this time to consider questions centered on cost, quality, and affordability. "The broader questions we will answer together are the following: To build our capacity to more fully realize our vision, what can we—as individuals, as departments, and as a campus community—do to build institutional value; that is, to improve our quality, manage costs, and remain affordable for the students and families we serve?" Johnson writes in a February 2013 memo to faculty and staff announcing the new round of visioning sessions.

Informal small group discussion centered on questions like: How do you think of quality as it relates to the work you do at Finlandia? What kinds of things could easily, immediately, and cost-effectively boost Finlandia's quality? What do you think contributes most substantially to the cost of the type of college education that Finlandia offers? What is your area doing now to manage costs? What trends, opportunities, and challenges do you see for Finlandia?

"These two encompassing series of conversations—more than 45 sessions to date—are providing a foundational shared language as we envision Finlandia's preferred future and her capacity to meaningfully realize that future," Johnson notes.

Precise and imaginative articulation; disciplined and innovative application; rigorous and continuous assessment of a clear and compelling vision: It is Johnson's conviction that as these three fundamental activities are pursued and accomplished, Finlandia's best self will emerge, flourish, and endure.

"When such is achieved, vision becomes our collective breath, our very life source," Johnson says of the three core pursuits. In other words, the resulting 2014 to 2021 strategic planning document "becomes that singular lens through which we view the entirety of our life together. It becomes our reason for being. It defines us, unites us, inspires us and, ultimately, sets us apart. This is the task before us. This is our calling, our vocation."

"It is clear from the visioning conversations that Finlandia's learning community—faculty, staff, students, community members, and stakeholders—hold strong convictions about student learning and growth, institutional identity and distinction, and community engagement," Johnson notes.

President Johnson congratulates 2013 B.F.A. graduate Sascha Hirzel.

Tomoyuki Ishizuka, A.G.S.

"Our learning community voices an equally strong conviction that Finlandia's value and success—past, present, and future—has been and must continue to be built upon her people and her academic programs.

"Finlandia faculty and staff are interested in the whole student and in academic programs and curricula that blend the expansive character of a liberal arts education with the subject mastery and professional proficiencies required during and beyond college life.

"But it's Finlandia's institutional posture of uncommon attention that holds the greatest value in the mind of each member of our learning community," Johnson concludes. "With an individualized blend of challenge and support, Finlandia faculty and staff want to continue accompanying our students on their journeys toward academic success and personal growth."

This season of focused strategic visioning and thinking will continue at Finlandia through January 2014. Though still being revised, President Johnson offers the following sample of the emerging visioning language.

Dawn Hilts, B.F.A.

Eric Hinsch, B.F.A.

Kailee Laplander, B.A.

To Embrace and Evolve our Distinctives. We will authentically embrace and more deliberately evolve our distinctives in order that Finlandia University be a place both rooted and relevant, both distinctive and inclusive. What does this mean?

- It means that Finlandia University will embrace and embody in campus life and learning those ideas and ideals championed in Finnish and Finnish American cultural expression that enrich student life, encourage student growth, and promote academic success.

- It means that Finlandia University will embrace and embody abiding values offered in Lutheran higher education that invite students to embark on both an inward and outward journey during college and beyond: seizing life as a calling; an openness to all; the free and fearless pursuit of all knowledge and all ways of knowing; service to neighbor; working for peace and justice; and caring for the earth.

- It means that Finlandia University will engage in continuous and comprehensive reflection to ensure missional integrity and innovation.

To Engage and Accompany—as a Whole Community—the Whole Student. We will offer a community-centric higher education experience that is relationship-driven, holistic, and transformative: Human Higher Ed. What does this mean?

- It means that teaching and learning at Finlandia University will be a shared and integrated enterprise: a whole community accompanying the whole student.

- It means that teaching and learning at Finlandia, both traditional and digital, will be anchored in human interaction and community.

- It means that teaching and learning at Finlandia University will recognize students as whole persons and will engage and accompany them in mind, heart, and body.

- It means that teaching and learning at Finlandia University will be for the purpose of human growth and transformation that leads toward a deeper understanding of the wider world and the consequential life.

Class of 2013 nursing graduates (left to right): Katie Frederick, Tricia Daavettila, Amy Crick, Elizabeth Corrigan, Kaitlin Codere-Lanouette, Jesse Cleaver, and Kendra Benson.

To Enrich and Advance Neighboring Communities.
We will lead with others to create conditions in which neighboring communities can grow and thrive. What does this mean?

- It means that Finlandia University will imagine and model shared practices that ensure sustainably robust campuses and communities.

- It means that Finlandia University will champion diverse human expressions and experiences on campus and in surrounding communities.

- It means that Finlandia University will contribute to the economic well-being of the western Upper Peninsula of Michigan and beyond.

- It means that Finlandia University will continue to offer an affordable, independent, liberal arts-based higher education opportunity for students and families in the Upper Peninsula and beyond.

Johnson notes that the above sampling does not imply a new direction for Finlandia as much as it provides a framework and vocabulary for a vision-framed plan that moves beyond institutional moorings, such as enrollment, governance, and finance.

"The need to strengthen these moorings, however, remains in view even as we chart a course toward Finlandia's 125th birthday," Johnson adds. "Though great strides have been made during Finlandia's current five-year plan—a plan centered on strengthening her institutional moorings—work remains to be done. We will continue to review these goals and adjust our strategies in this new season of planning. Yet, Finlandia's best self lies deeper within and we must pursue this more deliberately. I believe that when we more clearly articulate and purposefully pursue a shared vision, Finlandia's institutional moorings will be strengthened and her value in higher education will be enhanced."

Photo by Adam Johnson.

Campus and Community: Together for Good

Building on the commitments within the Campus and Community: Together for Good partnership and the capital initiatives which it has enabled, Finlandia will continue to seek new and more effective strategies for achieving enrollment growth, diversity, and quality through both curricular and co-curricular development.

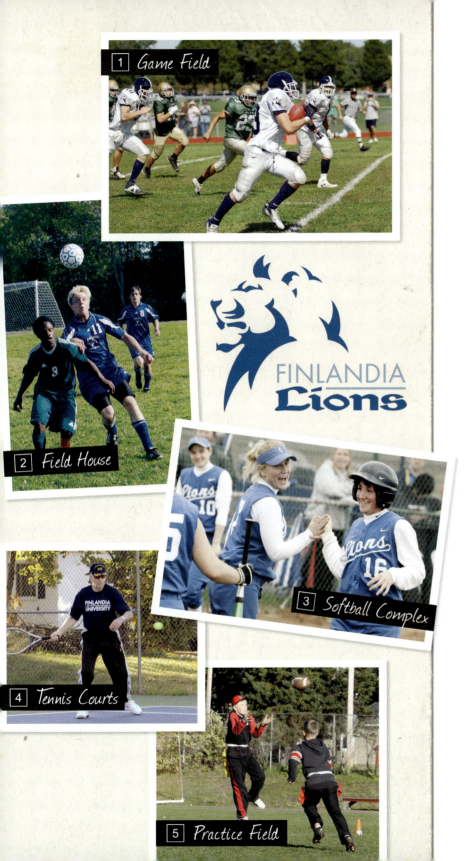

1. Game Field
2. Field House
3. Softball Complex
4. Tennis Courts
5. Practice Field

The Finlandia University Athletic Complex

The fall 2011 completion of McAfee Field represents a significant milestone in building a first-class NCAA Division III collegiate athletic program. When strategic athletic program additions are complete, it is projected that Finlandia's student-athlete population will increase 85 percent (from 178 in fall 2010 to about 330). Further, in the same period the ratio of student-athletes to the general student population is expected to increase from 30 percent to 40 percent.

President Johnson understands that co-curricular program development—such as NCAA Division III athletics—is as much a missional commitment as it is a strategy for enrollment. "The student-athlete-focused philosophy of NCAA Division III athletics fully complements Finlandia's vision for accompanying the whole student toward academic achievement and personal growth," Johnson explains. "I have witnessed the transformative potential of collegiate athletics in the lives of our student-athletes. A thriving, robust athletics program is, I believe, essential for achievement of Finlandia's vision for enrollment growth, quality, and diversity."

McAfee Field, the first phase in construction of the Finlandia University Athletic Complex, was funded by major gifts to the "Hear Our Roar" capital campaign, which continues. Future plans for the athletic complex include a 25,000 square-foot "Lion's Den" field house—with locker rooms, offices, conference and training rooms, and a sports medicine suite—to better serve the existing Finlandia sports programs of soccer, softball, and cross country, and to accommodate new ones, such as football and tennis. Additional components will include bleacher grandstands, a regulation softball field and dugouts, a training field, a nature trail, and an open air pavilion and picnic area.

Photo by Adam Johnson.

The College of Health Sciences

The second property acquired in the Campus and Community: Together for Good exchange is the historic Hancock High School, a four-story, 73,000 square foot educational facility located directly adjacent to the university's campus on Hancock's main thoroughfare. This iconic Hancock landmark will become the new home of Finlandia's College of Health Sciences.

Anchored by the university's nursing program, the new home of the College of Health Sciences will be a state-of-the-art facility capable of serving a health sciences student population of more than 300. The facility will also provide program and facility resources for community health care providers, and expand Finlandia's outreach capacity with enhanced and expanded community and co-curricular spaces.

Renovation plans include new classrooms well-equipped with instructional technologies, health science skill labs, a virtual lab equipped with patient simulators, computer labs, a large conference room, a community and student resource-training center, a student lounge, and faculty and staff offices.

Johnson believes that renovation of this historic building, once realized, will have a transformational impact on Finlandia and its neighboring communities. "The new physical plant for the College of Health Sciences will heighten the degree of excellence already demonstrated by Health Sciences faculty, programming, and graduates," Johnson says. "And it will strengthen Finlandia's long-standing commitment to prepare competent and compassionate health care workers for the Upper Peninsula and beyond."

Commitments guiding Finlandia's renovations to the historic Hancock High School building include the creation of a thoroughly collegiate environment; preservation of the historic character of the building, where possible; and the enhancement of spaces for community use.

Artist renderings of the future home of the Finlandia University College of Health Sciences.

Bibliography

Heikkinen, Jacob W. *The Story of the Suomi Synod: The Finnish Evangelical Lutheran Church of America, 1890-1962*. New York Mills: self-published, 1985.

Holmio, Armas K. E. *History of the Finns in Michigan*. Trans. Ellen M. Ryynanen. Detroit: Wayne State University Press, 2001.

Jalkanen, Ralph J., ed. *The Faith of the Finns: Historical Perspectives on the Finnish Lutheran Church in America*. Lansing: Michigan State University Press, 1972.

-----. *The Finns in North America: A Social Symposium*. Hancock: Michigan State University Press for Suomi College, 1969.

-----. *The Way It Was: Memories of the Suomi Synod*. Hancock: Suomi College, 1990.

Niemi, Les. *Memories: The Life and Two-Pronged Ministry of Les Niemi*. Self-published, 2012.

Wargelin, John. *The Americanization of the Finns*. Hancock: The Finnish Lutheran Book Concern, 1924.

Suomi College. *Suomi-Opiston Albumi*, 1896-1906. Hancock, 1906.

Suomi College, *Fennia* Yearbook. Hancock, 1915.

Suomi College, *Suomi* Yearbook. Hancock, 1916, 1917, 1919, 1920-1922, 1924, 1926, 1927, 1931, 1932, 1934-1936.

Suomi College. *Fiftieth Anniversary Publication of Suomi College and Theological Seminary 1896-1946*. Hancock: Finnish Lutheran Book Concern, 1946.

Suomi College. *Analogue* Yearbook. Hancock, 1948.

Suomi College. *Suomian* Yearbook. Hancock: 1949-1958, 1960, 1961, 1963-1969, 1970-1976, 1978, 1979, 1980-1986.

Suomi College. *Inklings* periodic student newspaper. Hancock, 1939-1971.

Suomi College. *The Bridge* periodic magazine. Hancock, 1976-1999.

Suomi College. *Suomi College: A Century of Opportunity Centennial Book*. Hancock, 1996.

Finlandia University. *The Bridge* periodic magazine. Hancock, 2000-2012.

Photography Credits

Unless otherwise noted, all photographs and images in this publication are the property of Finlandia University or the university's Finnish American Historical Archive. All rights, including those of duplication, are reserved in full by the University and the Archive.

Appendix
A university overview

FINLANDIA UNIVERSITY
Finlandia University was founded as Suomi College in 1896. It is a not-for-profit, co-educational liberal arts college affiliated with the Evangelical Lutheran Church in America (ELCA). Finlandia is the only private college in Michigan's Upper Peninsula and the only institution of higher learning in North America founded by Finnish immigrants.

Our Location. Finlandia's campus is in Hancock, Michigan, on the Keweenaw Peninsula, which is the northernmost point of land in Michigan.

Our Mission. Finlandia University is a learning community dedicated to academic excellence, spiritual growth, and service. The university fosters intellectual challenge, open dialogue, service to others, and an entrepreneurial response to a world characterized by change.

ACCREDITATION
Finlandia University is accredited by the Higher Learning Commission of the North Central Association for Colleges and Schools (NCA-HLC). For more information, visit the HLC-NCA on-line at www.ncahlc.org.

The Finlandia University baccalaureate nursing program is accredited by the Commission on Collegiate Nursing Education, One Dupont Circle, NW, Suite 530, Washington DC 20036, (202)887-6791, and approved by the Michigan State Board of Nursing of the Michigan Department of Consumer & Industry Services, Board of Nursing, P.O. Box 30193, Lansing, MI 48909, (517) 335-0918.

The Finlandia University physical therapist assistant associate in applied science program is accredited by the Commission on Accreditation in Physical Therapy Education (CAPTE), 1111 North Fairfax Street, Alexandria, Virginia 22314; telephone: 703-706-3245; email: accreditation@apta.org; website: http://www.capteonline.org.

The Finlandia University certified medical assistant associate in applied science program is accredited by the Commission on Accreditation of Allied Health Education Programs (www.caahep.org) upon the recommendation of the Medical Assisting Education Review Board (MAERB). Commission on Accreditation of Allied Health Education Programs, 1361 Park Street, Clearwater, FL 33756, 727-210-2350.

FINLANDIA UNIVERSITY INSTITUTIONAL MEMBERSHIPS
- Association of Governing Boards (AGB)
- Association of Independent Colleges and Universities of Michigan (AICUM)
- Council for Higher Education Accreditation (CHEA)
- Council of Independent Colleges (CIC)
- Keweenaw College Access Network
- Keweenaw Peninsula Chamber of Commerce
- Lutheran Educational Conference of North America (LECNA)
- Michigan Campus Compact (MCC)
- National Association of Independent Colleges and Universities (NAICU)

STUDENT DEMOGRAPHICS
Fall 2012
- 570 students
- 60% women, 40% men
- 11:1 student-to-faculty ratio
- Average class size is 14 students
- 75% are pursuing bachelor degrees
- 26% live on campus
- 14% are from other U.S. states
- 16% are minority students
- 5% are international students
- 60% to 70% of all Finlandia students are PELL-eligible

DEGREES AND AREAS OF STUDY
Bachelor of Arts
Majors: Art Therapy, Communication, Criminal Justice, English, History, Liberal Studies, Pre-professional Science, Psychology, Social Sciences, Sociology

Bachelor of Business Administration
Majors: Accounting, Applied Management, Arts Management, Business Management, Healthcare Management, International Business, Marketing, Sports Management

Bachelor of Fine Arts
Concentrations: Ceramic Design, Graphic Design/Digital Art, Fiber/Fashion Design, Integrated Design-Product/Interior/Sustainable, Studio Arts-Illustration/Drawing and Painting

Bachelor of Science in Nursing
Majors: Nursing, RN-to-BSN Completion

Associate in Applied Science
Majors: Certified Medical Assistant, Criminal Justice, Physical Therapist Assistant

Associate of Arts

Associate in General Studies

English as a Second Language Certificate Program

FINLANDIA UNIVERSITY VALEDICTORIANS, 1999 TO 2013

1999: Sheila Tormala
2000: Jordan Kivela
2001: Shelley Sivonen
2002: Jennifer Wilson and Jayne Fredrick
2003: Lillian Sederholm and Wendy Backus
2004: Toni Strutz and Denise Staricha
2005: Robin Dueweke and Karen Heck
2006: Kasey Engman
2007: Nora Hyrkas
2008: Nancy Lynn Kauppila
2009: Lauren VanderLind
2010: Meisha Bray
2011: Adam Jeffrey and Amanda Moyer
2012: Dawn Engman
2013: Eric Hinsch

FINLANDIA UNIVERSITY ATHLETICS

Finlandia University intercollegiate athletic programs encourage personal growth, academic success, and the development of athletic skills. Finlandia University does not offer athletic scholarships.

Affiliations and Conferences
- National Collegiate Athletic Association Division III (NCAA DIII)
- Association of Division III Independents (AD3I)
- Great South Athletic Conference (GSAC): Women's Softball
- Midwest College Hockey Association (MCHA): Men's Hockey
- Northern Collegiate Hockey Association (NCHA): Women's Hockey
- Wisconsin Intercollegiate Athletic Conference (WIAC): Men's Soccer

The Finlandia Lions compete as an independent institution in the sports of: Men's and Women's Basketball, Cross Country, and Golf; Women's Soccer and Volleyball; and Men's Baseball.

Athletic Programs
- Fall: Women's Volleyball; Women's and Men's Soccer, Cross Country, and Golf
- Winter: Women's and Men's Basketball and Hockey
- Spring: Women's Softball and Men's Baseball

Finlandia University Men's and Women's Athletics Records, 1999 to 2013
- Bill Loeks - 2000-01 NSCAA Men's Basketball All-American
- Beth Koski - 2003-04 USCAA Women's Basketball All-American
- Tyler Gordon - 2008 NCAA DIII Men's Basketball Steals Leader with 4.0 steals per game
- Tyler Gordon - 2009 AD3I Men's Basketball Player of the Year
- Tyler Gordon - 2010 NCAA DIII Men's Basketball Steals Leader with 3.6 steals per game
- Brittany Garland - 2011 NCAA DIII Softball Run's Batted In Leader with 2.08 RBI per game
- Brittany Garland - 2011 AD3I Women's Softball Player of the Year
- Shawn Hendrickson - 2011 AD3I Women's Softball Coach of the Year
- India Slayback – 2011 AD3I Women's Softball Rookie of the Year
- Gerard Taylor - 2011 AD3I Men's Baseball Rookie of the Year
- 2000-01 Men's Basketball NSCAA National Champions
- 2003-04 Women's Basketball USCAA National Champions
- 2006-07 Men's Hockey MCHA Tournament Champions
- 2011-12 Women's Softball 26-8 overall record, a winning percentage of .765 which is the best in program and school history
- 2012-13 Women's Softball first-ever Great South Athletic Conference (GSAC) Title
- 2013 Women's Softball first-ever NCAA Division III Regional Tournament appearance

Men's and Women's Basketball 1,000 Point Club

Name	Academic Year	Team	Total Points
Tyler Gordon	2006-10	Men's B-ball	1743 points
Beth Koski	2000-04	Women's B-ball	1687 points
Ryan Artley	2003-06, 07-08	Men's B-ball	1593 points

Tyler Lloyd	2002-06	Men's B-ball	1455 points
Mike O'Donnell	1999-2004	Men's B-ball	1320 points
Ally Tincknell	2006-10	Women's B-ball	1249 points
Jodi Riutta	2006-10	Women's B-ball	1190 points
Jacob Polfus	2000-04	Men's B-ball	1098 points
Delsie Luokkala	2000-04	Women's B-ball	1080 points
Victor Harrington	2003-05, 06-07	Men's B-ball	1073 points
Nick Forgette	2000-04	Men's B-ball	1043 points

Suomi College Athletics Records, 1964 to 1981
National Junior College Athletic Association (NJCAA)
All-Region XIII Honorees

Men's Basketball:

Year	Name	Additional Awards
1964	Charles Smith	
1965	Dan Sutton	
1967	Dave Vertanen	
1969	Gene Aho	
1970	Chuck Finkbeiner	1971 Region MVP
1970	Larry Dunklee	Ranked 14th in nation for Field Goal Percentage at 59.7%
1973	Tom Johnson	
1979	Ernest Montgomery	"All-American" honors
1980	Matt Johnson	
1981	Kenny Williamson	

Women's Basketball
1981-82   Team Record of 16-4   NJCAA Region XIII Runners Up

Finlandia University and Suomi College Presidents
1896-1919: J. K. Nikander
1919-1927: John Wargelin
1922-1923: Minnie Perttula-Maki
1927-1930: Antti Lepisto
1930-1937: John Wargelin
1937-1947: Viljo K. Nikander
1947-1949: Carl Tamminen
1949-1952: Bernhard Hillila
1952-1954: Edward J. Isaac
1954-1959: David Halkola
1959-1960: Raymond G. Wargelin
1960-1990: Ralph J. Jalkanen
1990-1991: Sidney Rand
1991-2007: Robert Ubbelohde
2007-present: Philip R. Johnson

Finlandia University Board of Trustees
As of January 1, 2013
John H. Stierna (Chair)
Julie Badel (Vice Chair)
Jane M. Lepisto (Secretary)
Kenneth D. Seaton (Treasurer)
Donald W. Bays
Kristin Hebrank
Ronald P. Helman
Lauri J. Isaacson (ex-officio)
Alice M. Kellogg
Jeanne Kemppainen
Paul Knuti
Michael A. Lahti
John M. Leinonen
John J. Perras
Eric W. Sauey
Luanne M. Skrenes
Patricia Van Pelt
Iola Jean Vanstrom
Peter A. Vorhes

Emeritus Members of the Board of Trustees
As of January 1, 2013
Samuel S. Benedict
Norman A. Berg
Willard L. Cohodas
John C. Hamar
Ray M. Hirvonen
Ronald D. Jones
Rudolph Kemppainen
Paavo Kortekangas
Richard T. Lindgren
Alexander McAfee
Ruben H. Nayback
Edith M. Niederer
Norma R. Nominelli
Dale R. Skogman
J. Philip Smith
Rollo Taylor
Alpo J. Tokola
Roger D. Westland

President's Circle
As of June 30, 2012

Lifetime membership in the President's Circle is granted to those who have given $50,000 or more to Finlandia University during any five-year period, and to those who have named the university in their estate plans for $50,000 or more and informed the university of their intentions. The list excludes deceased President's Circle donors and entities which no longer exist.

Reino E. Alanen
Trudy J. Alter
Dale W. App
Samuel and Elinor Benedict
Norman and Sharon Berg
Oscar and Patricia Boldt
David and Elsa Brule
Albert W. Cherne Foundation
Willard and Lois Cohodas
Coleman Foundation
Tauno Ekonen
Gordon W. Elson
Evangelical Lutheran Church in America
Ford Motor Company Fund
Allen K. Freis
Rollin M. Gerstacker Foundation
John Good
John and Joan Hamar
Arvo and Laila Heino
Philip Hillmer
Ray and Rachel Hirvonen
David and Patricia Holli
William Jackson
KEK Family Limited Partnership (Rautiola Family)
W.K. Kellogg Foundation
Rudolph and Darley Kemppainen
Leroy R. Keranen
John and Pauline Kiltinen
Sylvi Kivikoski
Michael and Sharon Lahti
Nancy Lematta
Raymond and Lois Lescelius
Richard and Lois Lindgren
W.W. Finny and Stella Martin
Roger and Karen Mattson
Alexander McAfee
McGregor Fund
Ruth E. Morgan
Carl O. Nelson
Edith M. Niederer
Leslie and Marcia Niemi
Kathryn R. Olson
Arlene and Forrest Winston Page Foundation
Paloheimo Foundation
John and Pamela Perras
Dale and Lorena Quasius
June Rawl
Retirement Research Foundation
William and Floy Sauey
Kenneth Seaton
Lois Shelton
Siebert Lutheran Foundation, Inc.
John and Roma Siller
Dale and Josephine Skogman
Superior National Bank
Thrivent Financial for Lutherans
Alpo and Bobbie Tokola
Harry A. and Margaret D. Towsley Foundation
Robert and Susan Ubbelohde
Upper Peninsula Power Company / WPS Resources Foundation, Inc.
Neal and Iola Jean Vanstrom
Samuel L. Westerman Foundation

Honorary Doctoral Degrees Awarded by Suomi College and Finlandia University
1994: Andrea Hauge-Bacon, Greta Peck
1995: F. Donald Kenney, Leonora Paloheimo, E. Olaf Rankinen
1996: Paavo Kortekangas, Aileen Maki, Ellwood Mattson, Kenneth Seaton
1997: Willard Cohodas, James Derse, Karlo Keljo, Riita Uosukainen
1998: Jaan Kiivit, John Vikstrom, Hikaru Yamamoto
1999: Martti Ahtisaari
2000: Jean Drey, Charles Gebhardt, Herman Gundlach, Paavo Lipponen, Dale Skogman
2001: Tarja Halonen, Jorma Ollila
2002: H. George Anderson, Andrew Wisti
2003: Gloria Jackson
2004: Aatos Erkko, Rudolph Kemppainen, Norma Nominelli
2005: Antti Lepisto, Jukka Valtasaari
2006: John Hamar, David Tiede, Matti Vanhanen, Donald Wanhala
2008: Pekka Lintu
2009: Peter Van Pelt
2010: Bishop Alex Malasusa
2011: Barbara Barrett
2012: Paul Halme
2013: Elsa Brule